Managing
Information Systems
as a Corporate
Resource

Managing Information Systems as a Corporate Resource

John P. Murray

Dow Jones–Irwin
Homewood, Illinois 60430

© DOW JONES–IRWIN, 1984

All rights reserved. No part of this publication may be reproduced, stored in a retrieval system, or transmitted, in any form or by any means, electronic, mechanical, photocopying, recording, or otherwise, without the prior written permission of the publisher.

This publication is designed to provide accurate and authoritative information in regard to the subject matter covered. It is sold with the understanding that the publisher is not engaged in rendering legal, accounting, or other professional service. If legal advice or other expert assistance is required, the services of a competent professional person should be sought.

From a Declaration of Principles jointly adopted by a Committee of the American Bar Association and a Committee of Publishers.

ISBN 0-87094-428-2

Library of Congress Catalog Card No. 83-70876

Printed in the United States of America

1 2 3 4 5 6 7 8 9 0 K 1 0 9 8 7 6 5 4

Dedication

This book is dedicated to my wife. Without her patience, understanding, and support, the project never would have been completed.

Preface

This book is about the growing issues which are involved in the management and continuing interaction of information processing within the context of the entire organization. The role of information processing has become so pervasive in all organizations that its management must not only improve, but must also come to be much better understood throughout the entire organization.

The technology of information processing is changing completely every five years. Some of the work which can be accomplished through the efforts of the well-run information processing department today was not feasible, or even possible, even as little as five years ago. Advances in the technology, both hardware and software, coupled with dramatic decreases in cost (a result of new technology) have opened new areas. The next five years will see an even more dramatic increase in these opportunities.

As an example, five years ago the *microprocessor*, or personal computer, was only beginning to become available. It was, at that time, little more than a curiosity. Today, the personal computer has become a ubiquitous, powerful, very effective tool in many organizations. The introduction of the personal computer has, in addition to providing an alternative to the typical role of information processing, also presented (although it is not yet often recognized) a number of serious problems.

The issue of the personal computer is simply a microcosm of the other issues involved in the management of the information system function. The environment of information systems must be improved; people outside the function must better understand both the problems and the opportunities inherent in the function. The feeling that information processing is too complex, somehow too esoteric for those outside the information processing department to grasp, to fully comprehend, must, for the good of all concerned, be overcome.

It is the goal of this book to raise issues, to present solutions, which will not only help both those within and outside of information processing better understand, and ultimately better manage the information processing function, but also to encourage all concerned to give more thought to where their particular organizations are with information processing, and where they are going with the function. There can be no doubt, those organizations which do the best job with information processing will do the best job overall.

Contents

	Preface	vii
CHAPTER I.	Importance to Entire Organization of Management Information Services Function in the '80's	1
CHAPTER II.	The Effective Interaction Between MIS and its Clients	17
CHAPTER III.	The Automated Office	29
CHAPTER IV.	Preparing for a Data Processing Disaster	43
CHAPTER V.	Feasibility	55
CHAPTER VI.	State of the Art	65
CHAPTER VII.	The Information Center	83
CHAPTER VIII.	Project Management within the Management Information Services Department	103
CHAPTER IX.	The MIS Steering Committee	121
CHAPTER X.	The Concept of Data as a Valuable Organizational Resource	147
CHAPTER XI.	The Future	165
	Fixed Asset Accounting—Statement of Requirements July 14, 1981	175
	Cost Benefit Analysis—Fixed Asset Accounting System September 1981	183
	Index	191

CHAPTER I
Importance to Entire Organization of Management Information Services Function in the '80's

The growth of data processing, or as it is increasingly called, Management Information Services (MIS), is an expanding phenomenon in all organizations, irrespective of size. This is just as true for the smallest organization which has just taken delivery of its first small computer, as it is for the very large organization, with a myriad of computers, and all organizations in between these extremes. The rapid pace of this phenomenon will not slacken in the future; indeed it will quicken.

The expansion of the use of computers and the concomitant technological advances in both the hardware and the software has not been limited to the traditional data processing departments of organizations. The computer, in whatever form, be it a personal computer, a word processor, an electronic mail system, or a Cathode Ray Tube (CRT) linked to a large central processor has begun to invade all areas of organizations. The size of the organization is immaterial. Equipment is now available at prices which are so reasonable and which will continue to fall, that the smallest organization can afford to automate, indeed even the smallest organization cannot afford *not* to automate.

Indeed, this rush to the introduction of automation, or the vast expansion of current data processing capabilities is almost boundless. Because of the rapid changes in technology and of the growing awareness of the benefits of that technology, if appropriately managed and controlled, what are viewed as practical limits, both in capabilities and cost-justified approaches today in organizations, will seem to have been rather shortsighted several years in the future.

This growth will present new challenges, new opportunities, and new potential for failure. The intent of this book is to consider three areas of challenge, opportunity, and failure, in order to provide insight into the issues of improved management of information, and to recommend courses of action which can lead to success. The fact that such consideration is necessary is borne out by the current state of information processing in many organizations, which is, unfortunately, less than effective. An objective analysis of the empirical evidence of the results of MIS in many organizations during the past twenty years would not be particularly positive.

Twenty years of experience and observation have convinced the author that, provided strong, effective management is brought to the MIS function, the current and future opportunities inherent in information management can pay large dividends for any organization, regardless of size. The primary purpose of this book is to stress the importance of the opportunities available through the combination of the extant and developing technologies and appropriate management techniques. A concomitant purpose is to encourage everyone in the organization to adopt a willingness to accept a higher degree of risk in moving to new plateaus of organizational performance through the use of these techniques.

While there are almost unlimited opportunities in effective information management, there are also a number of real challenges which stand in the way of success. Because in many instances the traditional MIS approach has not produced complete results, specific attention will be paid to some of the areas of difficulty. Practical solutions will be offered which, if used, will produce solid (in some cases dramatic) results. These solutions are all drawn from practical experience (some of which, unfortunately, has been obtained at great personal cost). This is not a book of theory; everything recommended has been used, and has worked for the author. If some of the suggestions appear unorthodox, that may be, considering the track record of MIS, the reason why they have worked!

It should be noted, again, that size has little to do with the basic concerns of data processing, which are universal. There are no unique data processing problems! It is correct that, particularly with regard to the technology, specific concerns will differ. The problems encountered with the maintenance of a five-hundred CRT network are much more complex than that of a small installation of perhaps several *microprocessors* or a minicomputer. Yet the problems of service level, expense, vendor relationships, appropriate use of the technology, awareness of the continuing changes in the technology and how they will affect the organization, interaction with the data processing clients, system and programming and operational controls and overall results are, while the magnitude changes with the size of the organization, valid and real concerns whenever computers are in operation.

What this has come to mean then, in a practical sense, is that these concerns now span an almost unbelievable spectrum of business functions. Information management is no longer the private concern of the data processors (although many in data processing do not yet understand that the environment has changed), but it has become part of the daily business effort of everyone in the business world. Not everyone in an organization has the same needs or interests in the information, but everyone increasingly has greater need, greater interest. How organizations face up to these needs and interests and how successful they are in the overall management of their information will, to a great extent, determine the success or failure of those organizations.

There is no question that, through the utilization of sound management practices and effective MIS leadership, all MIS installations can be improved; that even the worst case situations (and there are a number around) can not only be improved, but brought to high standards of performance. It is quite appropriate to claim that the problems which organizations currently face with their MIS functions, and increasingly those which they will face in the future, are not the serious problems with the technology which they have been in the past, but are much more problems of management.

The growth of the use of data processing has caused considerable tension, and in many cases confusion and dismay in many organizations, be they large, medium, or small. The cause of much of this negative atmosphere rests with the manner in which the data processing function has been, and unfortunately, continues to be, managed. Yet even with the MIS problems faced in many organizations, the demand to develop new computerized approaches to organizational concerns, to produce answers, to obtain results more rapidly, to decrease costs, and subsequently to improve the organization's competitive position have impelled organizations of all sizes to adopt the tools of the information explosion.

This then can be seen as a recognition by nonMIS management that even though computerization extracts a price, not only in real expense, but also in physiological terms, it is simply too pervasive and potentially too valuable not to use the technology to push ahead. Those outside the MIS arena often find themselves in a "no win" situation, they want to realize the benefits, yet the concerns appear overwhelming.

There is an almost palpable desire in many organizations to use data processing technology, even when that technology is little understood, even given all the prior problems and disappointments. It is of great importance that this desire be satisfied, but that can only be accomplished through strong, effective leadership. While the ideal would be to have this happen as a result of a coalition of the organization's MIS management, the various

MIS department clients, and the organization's senior management, that is not often the case.

Often the progress, or lack of MIS progress, made within an organization is a direct result of the leadership demonstrated by the MIS management team. A strong, aggressive MIS management which is able to produce results and build credibility can, and usually will, carry the rest of the organization along. As progress is made, the above-mentioned alliance of the various management factions within the organization can be forced to move to increasingly improved use of the technology. Nothing success like success. In those organizations where a significant part of the MIS promise has been delivered, and there are a number of such situations, these alliances of all management groups can be seen to be developing.

Those members of MIS management who possess the vision, the drive, and the ability to sell the benefits of data processing must begin to take an aggressive stance which will assure that MIS begins to deliver the benefits which are now available. The future success of MIS, and to a very great extent, the success of the organization, rests with the competence, aggressiveness, and willingness of the MIS management group to accept a reasonable degree of risk in order to assist the organization in the achievement of its goals.

The increasingly lower cost of data processing, the increasing reliability of data processing hardware, advances in the ease of use of such equipment, and the plethora of high-quality, practical software packages available for computers of all sizes clearly means that the demand for computerized solutions to current and unforeseen business problems will accelerate. This means that opportunities to use computerization to help drive the business and to explore new areas of profitability are now practical, both from a technical and a financial standpoint.

Organizations must become more flexible and much better able to provide increased service to their customers. The use of well-designed management information systems are an important aspect of the movement to this increased flexibility and improved service. Part of the "value added" aspect of any product or service will come to be seen in the future as those improvements which can come about through increased automation in all areas.

These developments then make projects, which even a few years ago were considered either too technically esoteric and/or too costly to be practical, at least worthy of serious investigation, if not implementation. Based upon that which is now occurring, one can only speculate as to what will happen during the next five years. It would certainly appear to be appropriate to state that hardware costs will continue to decline, software of all types will improve, and MIS clients will become increasingly knowledgeable about, and eager for, data processing solutions to their problems.

However, it stands to reason that as information processing hardware increases in speed and capacity and as the cost/benefit ratio of the equipment becomes lower, new demands will arise which will mean increased operating software to handle these new demands. That software is certain to become increasingly complex, so that while the MIS clients will obtain many benefits, one of which will be reduced client complexity, the MIS department must become more proficient in their management of the technology.

Many organizations have not yet recognized these changes; these new advantages which exist for those who are willing to accept new challenges, who possess the fortitude to face some increased risks, and to stay the distance when that is required. While many organizations, for a variety of reasons, some real, some imagined, will not adopt these new approaches, those which do and which move aggressively to fully utilize the new technologies will emerge as clear winners. It should become increasingly apparent to anyone who gives the matter serious consideration that the time is now at hand for the MIS function to begin to move from the traditional "backroom" accounting and record-keeping functions to a much more usable and meaningful position within the organization.

This is not to imply that the rather mundane record keeping and accounting functions performed by the MIS departments are not important or not of value; those functions of course must continue, and must be of primary concern to the organization. In those organizations where these functions are not well managed, they must be improved. The goal should be to handle these functions in an efficient, almost routine manner so that MIS can begin to concentrate on those new areas where, through the use of the technology, an increasingly significant contribution to the growth of the organization can be made by MIS.

While many organizations have had MIS functions in existence for a considerable length of time, an objective analysis of the results produced, particularly compared to those promised, would demonstrate that the success and credibility records of MIS in many organizations have been less than outstanding. Too often the real potential of MIS has simply not been achieved.

Although it is correct that in many instances the MIS promise has not been delivered, and while every organization, no matter how effective its MIS function, can document at least several horror stories, a blanket condemnation of MIS would be patently unfair. There are a number of organizations which have done a very effective job in the development and continuing growth of their MIS function. These organizations must be recognized as having been able to produce excellent results and as having made significant contributions to their organization's bottom lines. Again, size has nothing to do with results, good or bad. Just as there are large, medium, and small MIS installations which have produced more chaos and confusion than benefit, so are there installations in each size category which have done an outstanding job.

Those organizations which have developed MIS functions which have delivered results simply attest to the fact that, given proper support and encouragement, appropriately managed and controlled, MIS can indeed become a driving force in the growth and effectiveness of the organization it seeks to support. Prior to the consideration of specific issues of effective MIS results, it may prove helpful to consider some of the more subtle factors which have helped produce those environments in which MIS has either been able to succeed, or has come to be something less than successful.

The typical organization suffers from what might be best described as a "cultural" problem between MIS and those it attempts to serve. This is a problem which has been recognized over the years and about which a great deal has been written. However, the effort to mitigate the problem, both within MIS and within the areas of the organization which use the services of MIS, has not been particularly successful.

It is not any secret that in most organizations the MIS function is not viewed as being an integral part of the rest of the organization. The impression, outside the MIS department, is that members of MIS use too much jargon, are much more concerned with the technology than with the interests of the organization, are unable or unwilling to relate to the "bottom line" issues of the organization, and that they often adopt an imperious attitude with those outside the MIS department. There is not any question that members of MIS have been guilty of all of the above.

However, the other side of that problem is that those outside the MIS department, including members of senior management, are often not willing to make a serious effort to understand the problems of the MIS department, to appreciate the complexities of the work, or to develop the basic knowledge which would enable them to provide effective help and guidance to the MIS effort.

As long as this cultural problem exists, the organization will not be able to obtain the real benefits of MIS. Clearly, work must be carried on to effect changes in the organizational climate which will engender a growing awareness on the part of all concerned with the aspirations and concerns of members of the other group.

A rather striking example of the phenomenon can be seen in the issue of the introduction of "personal" computers within an organization. Often various department managers have a real need to use some manner of data processing power to increase the productivity of their departments. These managers may have attempted to obtain help from MIS to solve these problems and have been told that such help, because of the already large MIS project backlog, was simply out of the question. Faced with such a situation, still acutely aware of the urgent requirement to overcome their particular problems, these managers have sought to bring in their own small computers in order to accomplish their goals.

While these efforts have often proved to be very successful, they have, in many organizations, increased the friction between MIS and these managers who have "gone their own way." This often leads to the imposition of policies which forestall the introduction of these small computers, and the managers of these departments are left with problems and no viable solutions. This only increases the hostility between MIS and its clients.

It may well be the introduction of personal computers within an organization or within a particular department may not be in the organization's best interest, in fact there are cases where such an introduction has gotten out of hand and caused more difficulty than benefit. However, in those organizations where MIS stands opposed to personal computers and offers no alternatives, the matter will always be resolved by resourceful managers, often at a disadvantage to all concerned. When presented with a "not never, but not now" ultimatum, managers will do whatever is necessary to solve their problems, with or without the concurrence of MIS.

There are a number of apparently well-managed MIS departments which are simply citadels to self-preservation. Usually through an effective program to cow the clients, often because the organization's senior management does not fully understand the issues and may indeed be too wary of the MIS function, the MIS manager, subtly to be sure, has been able to gain an inordinate amount of actual, if not official, power.

In these circumstances, the MIS manager sets the course of the organization in many areas. He decides what MIS projects will be worked on, what technology to use, who will be granted MIS favors, and who will not. While this may be good for the individual MIS manager, it is certainly not in the best interest of the organization. Many MIS installations then, tend to become walled cities, much more concerned with the status quo than with any effort to provide improved service to the MIS clients, to accept reasonable risk to make progress, or to develop a concern with the development of effective MIS leadership.

There are several factions within any organization which must be considered in the development of an effective effort to provide Management Information Services to the organization. In order to achieve a strong, effective, progressive, MIS function these factions must be recognized and managed in such a fashion to provide harmonious results. Each faction has a specific part to play. To the extent that their interests are not accommodated, either through the machinations of one of the factions, or simply as a result of their failure to comprehend the issues, their responsibilities and the potential benefits, one of the other factions, either through design or default, will step in to gain an unfair advantage.

These factions are comprised of senior management, the MIS department clients (those who avail themselves of the MIS services), the management of the MIS department, and those vendors who supply significant quantities of hardware and/or software to the organization. Each faction must play a distinct role in order to gain the most from the expense devoted to MIS. To the extent that these roles are not fulfilled, or are not properly managed, MIS will fail. In those organizations where MIS has been successful, it has been because these groups have been able to develop a working relationship, which has produced both understanding and an aggressive tension which has been a driving factor in the continuing development of improved MIS service.

While each faction does have a role to play which must fit into the overall information delivery mosaic, each faction has its personal interests to guard. It is not any easier for those outside MIS to consider the abandonment of their self-interest in order to promote the common good than it is for MIS. However, each group must begin and then continue to work as hard as possible to consider the overall organizational interests ahead of their own. If this can be done and if everyone can develop not only an interest, but also an empathy for the concerns of the other factions, everyone, the vendors included, will benefit in the long run.

The crucial faction (for the purpose of this dissertation not, as is often the belief of MIS management, to the absolute viability of the organization) is MIS management. This is the case not only with respect to that which MIS is able to accomplish, but also in consideration of that which MIS may fail to accomplish. To develop and maintain an effective MIS organization today, the MIS manager must, first of all, be a manager. While a familiarity with the technical aspects of MIS are important, they cannot be the overriding concern to the MIS manager. Too many MIS departments have delivered much less than their potential because the manager was a technician. While the manager may have been an excellent technician, that is not the skill needed to bring the MIS function to fruition. Technical skills can, and should, be developed in MIS technicians, not MIS managers.

When technicians masquerade as managers, what often occurs is the development of "elegant Band-Aids." That is, great amounts of time and energy are devoted to the development of highly complex, very technically challenging solutions to problems; when what are really required are more simple, more direct business answers. The technician/manager tends to see all solutions as technical solutions and often succumbs to the temptation to continue to develop his technical skills at the expense of the clients.

Perhaps the most common single failure in MIS is connected to the promotion of strong technicians to MIS managers, who then fail to relinquish their technical skill in order to grow as managers and administrators. This is not to state that good technicians can never become good managers, they can; but they must be willing to develop management skills. It does appear that those skills and interests which help assure success as a technician, tend, in many instances, to preclude success as a manager.

Of course, in small installations, because of staff limitations, the technical skill must be considered important because often the person who is the MIS manager is also the person with the most technical skill and experience. Even in these situations, too much emphasis on things technical by this person will produce unnecessary problems.

The manager of the MIS function must adopt a business, rather than a technical, approach to the role of MIS manager. There must be a willingness to seek out and try new approaches, to understand the business functions of the MIS client departments, to "sell" the MIS function, and to build a strong relationship with those MIS seeks to serve, while working with the vendor to find and deliver solutions to the client's problems. It is of considerable importance that the MIS manager be viewed outside the MIS department as a competent member of the organization's management team, not as a technician.

Members of senior management should make an effort to understand that which is being done within the MIS department. This does not by any means have to be in-depth knowledge, but should be something more than superficial. A mere familiarity with MIS terms is not enough. The enrollment in various seminars and sessions which can be provided by the organization's own MIS people can provide a general understanding of MIS. Presentations by the MIS management group can provide considerable knowledge about the MIS function within the organization. The expressed concern of senior management for jargon-free presentations can alleviate one of the more burdensome aspects of this effort for senior management.

The work being carried on in the typical MIS department of any organization of any size is so pervasive and of critical importance to that organization, that at least a degree of senior management awareness and attention to that effort is really mandatory. There must be a reasonable assurance that the work being done in MIS, the projects selected, and the sums to be spent have a "linkage" to the organization's goals. Questions about the impact of MIS, its direction for the future, and the appropriateness of the projects being developed must be raised by senior management and acceptable answers must be provided.

Given the tools and techniques available today, any project senior management may want can be delivered, provided sufficient time and money are available. Those who are familiar with MIS functions may take exception with such a statement, but it is a fact that there are MIS departments in operation today which can deliver on such a statement. Therefore, it becomes incumbent upon senior management to make known both its needs and those speculative areas where, unbeknown to senior management, MIS may be able to provide substantial help, perhaps at less cost in terms of time and money than may be anticipated.

Too often senior management abandons its responsibility to MIS. It is often the case that MIS obtains direct attention from senior management only as the result of some crisis situation. Perhaps some disaster has occurred which has risen to the executive level of the organization; or perhaps, as part of a cost reduction effort, the MIS budget is perceived as being "too large," and therefore "out of control." In these cases, MIS is on the defensive. That may be quite appropriate, given the circumstances, but senior management should adopt a real, ongoing interest in MIS. Critical questions should be asked, just as they are asked of other departments; accurate, understandable answers should be demanded, just as they are of other departments. When these answers are obtained, they should be carefully considered by the senior management group. MIS should not always be in a defensive position in its relations with the senior management group. Attention to MIS planning, to its work, its results, and its goals, particularly as those goals relate to the goals of the organization, should be forthcoming from senior management.

The role of the vendors must be carefully considered. Too often vendors have been able to secure an inordinate amount of senior management attention and support and, as a consequence, an inordinate amount of power within the organization. This is simply an abdication of responsibility on the part of senior management. To be effective, the MIS function must be managed by MIS management, not the vendor. When this situation arises, the solution to all problems tend to gravitate, as one might anticipate, to the use of those hardware and software solutions which can be supplied by the vendor.

These particular solutions may indeed be quite appropriate; however, they should be installed as the result of careful analysis of the problems they are intended to solve and of their effectiveness and cost, not as a capitulation to a particular vendor. Astute MIS managers will maintain a certain independence from the vendors, particularly with regard to operational concerns. While this may require some additional organizational expense for manpower and training, it is best in the long term.

The vendors can provide great assistance; and, where appropriate, their help should be solicited. This should always be done under the control of the MIS management. The guidance of the vendors, in the areas of new technologies in attempting to determine other results in new areas, can and should be encouraged. Acting as an advisor, being able to present new ideas, can prove to be most beneficial to the organization. The representatives of the vendors gain access to a number of installations and can usually call on people with considerable technical skill to address specific solutions to problems; this help should be accepted, provided it is clear to all involved that MIS, not the vendor, is in control.

There are numerous examples of situations where the vendor has gained control (covert, if not overt control) of the MIS direction of the organization. When this occurs it is usually the result of the vendor being able to fill an existing vacuum. The fault lies, not with the vendor, but with the management of the organization, both senior management and MIS management. The primary responsibility lies within MIS, due to its failure to provide effective leadership.

What is the role of the MIS clients in the effort to provide strong MIS performance? First, MIS clients must gain a better understanding of both the possibilities and the complexities of the MIS effort, and then must be willing to work with MIS to make the necessary progress. Second, in order to be successful, MIS clients must be willing to accept more prominent roles in the design, development, and continuing operation of those MIS systems which support their departments' efforts. Clients must work to do a better job to determine the types of information they require, and be willing to work with MIS to ensure that what they require is what is delivered.

As an example, in spite of the now commonly used term "Management Information Services," the typical MIS department provides for more "data" than "information." There appears to be rather a large amount of confusion, not only in MIS, but in the client departments, about the distinction between "data" and "information." Part of the problem rests with the continuance of policies, procedures, and systems of the late sixties and the seventies. The fact that little thought or attention has been given to this subject has caused it to go unnoticed. However, as pressure for the delivery of true information grows, the issue will become better focused.

Many people engaged in MIS sincerely believe they are producing information which has immediate value to the organization. The rather common situation is that the production of reams of paper are equated with the production of information. The delivery of vast amounts of paper does not necessarily constitute the delivery of information. If the "information" delivered must be reworked by the client in order to answer his questions, what has been delivered is clearly not "information," but data.

Advances in technology, such as improved operating software, excellent applications software packages, the introduction of Data Base Management Systems (DBMS) with their provisions for use of "nonprocedural" or "high-level" programming languages, coupled with much more sophisticated hardware and dramatic reductions in the per transaction cost of data processing (hardware cost reductions) have made the delivery of information, as opposed to data, much more practical and cost effective than even a few years ago. However, the availability of these options does not in any way guarantee they will be accepted or used by an organization. If the MIS department is not willing to set the direction away from data, then the clients must accept an active role in encouraging such a trend.

This really needs to be carefully thought through. The installation of the appropriate software and hardware will not, by itself, solve the problem. The production of large volumes of paper may, to some extent, be the symptom rather than the cause. Unless more attention is placed upon the design of systems which have as their purpose the production of information, little will be accomplished with the use of advanced technology. The paper volume may be removed, but it will only be replaced with a data clutter produced on CRTs or microfiche.

An example of this difficulty of confusing data with information may provide some insight into the problem. One aspect of the movement from a "data" to an "information" environment would be to encompass the creation of more "exception reporting." That means the movement to an environment which, while it captures and if necessary can produce the data, the emphasis is to eliminate the routine use of that data and to concentrate on the production of meaningful information.

To illustrate, an organization's sales management may be presented each month with voluminous computer listings which show the organization's sales results. These listings may record, in great detail, data which shows sales by region, territory, salesman, customer, and product line. All of the data has some value, of course; however, the sales department management may have become so burdened with the detail they cannot properly focus on their real objective, improved sales. The sales managers may have to go through this mass of information to determine who is not up to quota, what lines are not selling well, and where sales are up. In fact, it may be that someone, perhaps several people, recap the computer produced data into other reports.

Why not determine the really salient information required by the sales department and produce reports, directly from the computer, which show that information? Perhaps limits should be determined, say any salesman with sales of ten percent plus or minus quota should be printed, all others will not be shown. The same limits could be set for region, territory, customer, or product line. The savings, in terms of processing time, paper, paper handling, and clerical effort (often being done by managers who should be managing) can be significant in organizations of any size.

Taking the example one step farther, making the information available on line, through the use of a Cathode Ray Tube (CRT) so that these managers can arrange and access the data to obtain immediate answers to their questions is a step forward in the movement to a true information environment. While this will no doubt seem elementary to those who have been associated with organizations which have made a concerted effort to deliver information, there are a large number of organizations which have not yet begun the process and such examples may prove helpful.

The reduction of the paper flow from MIS to the client departments should be a top priority for all MIS departments. There has been a great deal of unrest within client departments about moving to on-line systems, often because these clients have not felt they have had control over the environment. The MIS departments arranged the data, provided the CRT displays, and formatted the reports. The clients would accept the CRTs, but they often, and in many organizations probably still do, continue to get and to use the large volume paper reports. The new techniques available as adjuncts to the Data Base Management Systems provide the environment where the client can be in complete control. When this is correctly handled and actively pushed by the MIS department, the resistance will soon dissolve.

The blame for a lack of progress in the drive to move an organization from a data to an information environment does not rest entirely with the MIS department. It has only been in the last few years that high quality tools, techniques, and lowering costs have made the approach practical. However, the climate has changed; progressive MIS departments must begin to encourage these changes.

There are some political roadblocks. Often where such an approach is suggested, the MIS clients will be the ones who will object to the change. Many times these people see the large amounts of data they receive as "security blankets," and they will be reluctant to give them up. There are also instances where those receiving large volumes of data see that as a source of power or prestige, and they may be unwilling to admit they can make do with less. It is not at all unusual to question people in client areas about the use of specific reports to find that the answers received are often rather vague. They may not even have a use for the report; but because their predecessor received it, they are reluctant to give it up.

It is also correct that the MIS clients are often suspicious of the value of the data being produced by the MIS department. If the MIS department has a history of producing incomplete, inaccurate, or incorrect data, it will be that much more difficult to convince the clients that they should be satisfied to move to an exception-reporting environment.

There is another important aspect which must be considered because of the prominent position it occupies in the issue of developing an information environment. Most organizations have a significant investment in their MIS systems. The investment is not only financial (which may represent a considerable sum), but it is also emotional. The emotional involvement will not only be in the MIS department, where many of the people may have spent considerable time building and operating the systems, but the MIS client departments will also have become familiar with these systems and will therefore be reluctant to make changes.

The issue transcends the question of the production of information. Given both the potential and actual significance of the typical MIS function, little has been accomplished to effectively integrate the MIS effort into the mainstream of the organization. In many organizations the MIS emphasis has been to react, rather than to act. Too much crisis management exists in MIS departments. The impetus for a much-improved management prospective on the part of MIS management must begin.

While this impetus should ideally begin within the MIS department, it is unlikely to spontaneously occur in those departments where it is most needed. In many organizations this change will have to come from somewhere else, from senior management, or from the efforts of the MIS clients, or (worst case) the vendors, yet it must occur. The stakes are simply too high, the risks of not moving forward too great not to begin and to continue a sound, effective program from which an information environment can be built. Those organizations which ignore this issue, or which continue to procrastinate may find, relative to their competition, they have gotten too far behind to remain in the race.

These are by no means easy issues, they require commitment, planning, time, money, patience, and a willingness to stay the course. MIS departments, unfortunately, often view such issues in a negative light; they are considered too high risk, requiring too much hard work, and they may indeed result in a reduction of MIS control and power. In those organizations where the MIS management has held steadfastly to the more traditional approach of building ever larger staffs and ever more convoluted systems, movement to such new environments will be seen, not as exciting and rewarding for all concerned, but as a threat to the established MIS order.

However, progressive MIS departments have been able to move from the position of being large, high-speed accounting machines to becoming in effect, Information Utilities. It does require the acceptance of risk, it does entail many changes throughout the organization, and it may mean a diminution of the power of the MIS department, yet it must happen.

In well-managed, progressive MIS departments the function is beginning to move from the role of record keeper, or rather that role while still being accommodated is being accorded less importance than the development of the role of information provider. While the important record-keeping functions are being handled in a rather routine manner, the MIS manager can now begin to move the organization in new directions.

The introduction of the "Computer Utility" is now becoming a reality in some organizations. The ability of organizations to use computers to develop "what if" scenarios to make accurate forecasts and projections, based upon large amounts of data is coming increasingly into use. Automation in new, esoteric areas, such as teleconferencing, computer-assisted design, robotics, paperless order transmission, and invoicing, just to site a few examples, are increasingly coming into use. They cannot be effective if the basic MIS function is not well managed, and if the MIS management does not possess the vision to push the organization to these new environments.

As this occurs, the MIS function's linkage to the organization's bottom line will become increasingly apparent. While this will require a great deal of work in some organizations (in some it will be a horrendous task), it simply has to occur It must begin with a reorientation of the mission of the MIS function.

There is risk, of course. The degree of risk depends upon the current state of the organization's MIS environment. In all cases, the tools and techniques are available which, if used in conjunction with sound planning, control, and management, will hold risk to a reasonable level.

There are several key issues. There must be an awareness of the benefits available today from a good MIS function; it must be understood that, in many organizations a strong commitment, cultural changes, and leadership are necessary; it must also be understood that time, patience, and money will be required. The place to begin is with a review of the current MIS function and the MIS environment within the particular organization. An objective analysis of the strengths and weaknesses of the function must be carried on, so that, once there is an understanding of the current status of MIS, effective planning can be instituted to move to a much more effective function.

The purpose of this book then is to raise some of the important nontechnical issues and to help provide insight into those issues and then suggest practical, workable solutions. The task, even in well-run MIS departments is never easy; in poorly run departments it may border upon stupendous, yet it must be done.

This book will present a general overview of the information concerns of organizations. It is not focused upon any particular group; anyone with an interest in effecting improvements in information management, or in gaining improved insight into the more important information management issues, will find the material helpful. This interest and insight must become more pronounced, not only in MIS departments, but in all areas of the organization.

The issue of effective information management is so pervasive, so ubiquitous, so critical to the continued growth and health of all organizations, that it can no longer be left entirely in the hands of the organization's MIS professionals. Everyone, like it or not, is rapidly becoming increasingly involved in information management; the more attention everyone pays to the issues and to their solutions, the better it will be for our organizations.

This book has been prepared in the most jargon-free manner possible (a rather difficult task for a data processor) in order that readers lacking an in-depth knowledge of MIS can better understand both the issues and the solutions. There may appear to be recurrences of various themes and issues within the book; these do not indicate some inherent lack of discipline on the part of the author; they appear because it is of great importance that they be understood as being matters of significance.

It is possible the book will raise questions in the mind of the reader which will not be answered. The reader may take exception with some (perhaps many) of the points made in the book. If those circumstances do occur, the author does not view that as negative, anything which will increase thought about the effective management of information, which will help spur people to action, must be viewed as positive. Contentment with the status quo, or fear of change of information management within organizations, must not be allowed to continue.

CHAPTER II
The Effective Interaction Between MIS and its Clients

When considering the use of information processing, the primary emphasis is usually placed upon the tools and techniques, the hardware, the software, the system design, and programming considerations. There is no question that these are important aspects of information processing, and there should not be any doubt about the appropriateness of heavy emphasis on these aspects of the function. However, another important component (perhaps in the final analysis the most important component) of the eventual success or failure of the MIS function is often overlooked.

As the uses of the technology grow and become more varied, as new areas and new functions are automated, the necessity for increased recognition of the importance of building and maintaining sound relationships between MIS and those it serves, its clients, must be accorded increased prominence. Unless these relationships are given more attention, the real benefits to be realized through the use of the technology will be diminished. There are any number of organizations where the climate between the MIS department and those it should be seeking to serve is less than comfortable. There are some organizations where that climate can only be described as inimical.

These circumstances are of course unfortunate, if for no other reason than the simple fact that the time and energy devoted to inter- and often intradepartment hostility is time and energy which is lost to more productive endeavors. In those organizations where such situations exist, efforts must be undertaken to correct the problems. Unless action is taken to change the environment, it will only become worse. Those organizations which are free of such difficulties have come to that circumstance as a result of an ongoing effort to pay appropriate attention to these problems in order to make certain such situations do not develop.

Part of the problem rests in what might be best described as "cultural" differences. Usually those outside the MIS department do not sufficiently understand the function or appreciate the complexities of the MIS operation. Moreover, the MIS clients do not usually demonstrate any particular desire to learn more about the MIS function. It is also correct that, in many instances, the situation has often been exacerbated, to at least some degree, by an often imperious attitude on the part of many members of the MIS department. So long as such conditions are allowed to exist, the problems between MIS and its clients will not go away, nor will they become any less difficult.

It is not at all unusual to hear MIS clients complain about the quality of the work produced by the MIS department, about the uncooperativeness of the members of the MIS department, and about the repeated failures of MIS to deliver what it has promised. While there is often ample justification for such complaints on the part of MIS clients, the complaints are often made large by the clients because of personnel problems with the MIS department.

Conversely, members of the MIS department often feel that the clients do not appreciate that which is being done for them by MIS, that they are not aware of the hard work, and often long hours, which go into the MIS effort. Members of the MIS department also often feel that the demands being made upon them by members of the client departments are unreasonable, that too little thought is put into the requests which are presented to MIS for consideration, and that the deadlines for such requests are unrealistic.

Of course such attitudes tend to create barriers within the organization. MIS and the clients it should be attempting to serve often end up in accrimonious debate. Unless or until these barriers can be breeched, the results which should be forthcoming from MIS will not begin to be realized.

The development of strong, effective MIS/client relationships are critical for the development of a productive MIS effort. Today's MIS/client problems, if left unresolved, will become increasingly serious as those new technologies now being introduced in organizations place increasing responsibility for direct management of information in the client areas.

The solutions to most of the MIS/client problems are not complex or difficult. Improvements in these relationships can be effected in a rather short time, even in organizations where the climate has been allowed to badly deteriorate. In most instances, the effort to improve the MIS/client relationship must begin within the MIS department. There is no particular secret about the method which should be used to make improvements;

it is simply a matter of common sense, communication, and salesmanship. The practical MIS manager must develop a strong interest in improving the climate between MIS and its clients.

Why? If for no other reason than the very pragmatic one which is that there are many more clients throughout the organization than there are members of MIS. If the problems become too severe, sooner or later the matter will be brought to the level of senior management, if things grow too intense the usual solution to the problem (justified or not) is to replace the MIS manager. Therefore, if for no other reasons than those of self-interest, the MIS manager must take an active interest in the state of the MIS/client relationships and must work to make certain they become and remain good.

Typically, this problem of uneasy relationships is not restricted to the area of MIS and its departmental clients; it is also often a problem within the various sections of the MIS department. These internal MIS problems should not, as is often the case, be ignored. The build-up of friction within MIS has a detrimental effect on both the quality and the quantity of the work produced by the MIS department. This subject must be addressed in an active manner by the MIS manager, not only because it limits the effectiveness of the MIS function, but also because the ill will generated within the MIS department will infect the MIS/client relationships.

What often results in organizations where serious internal MIS discord is allowed to occur is that as the MIS service level falls and the ire of the MIS clients begins to grow, members of MIS tend to begin to blame those in other parts of the department for the problems. Such activity only makes matters more difficult for all concerned. The clients will often use the remarks made by members of one section of the MIS department as proof of the failure of members of another part of the department. This only increases the tension and makes matters worse for everyone.

It is of paramount importance, as a first step in the effort to improve the MIS/client relationship, that MIS internal discord be brought under control. The absolute reduction of all MIS internal friction is impossible, given the nature of the continuing pressures within the department. However, significant improvement can be achieved with appropriate MIS management attention.

One of the causes of internal MIS friction is the existence of what might be described as a "prima donna" syndrome. It is often the case that one or several individuals within the MIS department have been allowed over the years to run roughshod over everyone else in the department. These people can be found in any section of the department and they may be at any level. Usually they are very rigid and often unwilling to either cooperate or consider any position other than their own.

As long as this situation is allowed to continue, the climate within MIS will be unpleasant. How can the situation be resolved? Often MIS management will not take the necessary steps to correct the problem, because of a fear of losing a "valuable" employee. It simply has to be recognized that, in the final analysis, no employee is so valuable that they can be allowed to disrupt the department with impunity. Some corrective action must be taken. Employees who persist in being malcontent must be replaced.

An approach which moves to produce a "prima donna" free MIS department can produce a great deal of short-term trauma, yet in the long run, such an approach is the only effective method to employ. The change in atmosphere within an MIS department when the department becomes prima donna free can be dramatic.

While there are any number of reasons for the difficulty between MIS and its clients, there is a rather basic problem which often occurs. Many MIS employees tend to forget, or perhaps they never understand, that the primary mission of the MIS department is to provide support for the other departments of the organization. It often appears to those outside the MIS department that many of the people within the department feel that MIS is a function unto itself and that whatever occurs in other sections of the organization has little or no relationship to the MIS effort.

While the preceding impression may not be valid, in fact it often is not valid; too often members of MIS, albeit perhaps unintentionally, do convey the impression that they are somewhat different and, somehow better than others within the organization. The demand for the services of people with MIS skills has helped to foster such an attitude. It is a fact that in many instances, people in the MIS department are more interested in the development of their individual careers than in the long-term concerns of the organization which employs them. The high turnover rate among MIS people attests to this fact.

It is also apparent that members of MIS often hold a rather low opinion of others in the organization outside the MIS department. MIS clients are often treated by MIS employees in a manner which can only be described as arbitrary and imperious. This, of course, is a mistake; the MIS clients are not obtuse! While these clients may lack specific knowledge about the processes and technology of MIS, they do have an understanding of the business functions for which they are responsible, in all likelihood a better understanding than those in the MIS department with whom they are attempting to deal.

Rather than denigrate the competence of the MIS clients, members of MIS should work to get them on their side in order to help them develop an increased knowledge of the business side of the operation.

Those in MIS who will become successful in the future must develop increased business awareness and skills; a close association with those in the organization who understand the nonMIS business functions can help improve that awareness and those skills.

It would be impossible to estimate the amount of effort which is wasted, not to mention the actual harm caused organizations as a result of acrimonious relations between MIS and its clients (those MIS should be attempting to serve.) It is often overlooked that the time and energy devoted to heated debate, to attempts to fix blame, are time and effort which are being diverted from the real issue, which should be to concentrate on improved MIS service which can be used to help the entire organization make progress.

The success and continued growth of the MIS function and its contribution to the organization are contingent upon building and maintaining an environment which develops and nurtures both understanding and cooperation between MIS and its clients. This issue is too important to be ignored. The work carried on by MIS is too pervasive not to strive to make the results as beneficial to all as possible; whatever must be done to improve the MIS/client climate must be pursued.

Because of its position within the organization, because of the number of areas within the organization the MIS effort touches, MIS must take a leadership role in solving its image problems. Members of the MIS department, under the leadership of the MIS manager, must work hard to develop the appropriate sales and marketing skills which will help, not only improve its image within the organization, but, as an ancillary benefit, also begin to improve the quality of the work delivered by MIS. While many members of the MIS department will find the concept of "selling" both the MIS service and themselves somewhat onerous, it is a valid concept and one which must be pursued if the potential of the MIS effort is to be realized.

The effective MIS manager of the future (starting today) must become more of a salesman than is currently the case. At least a portion of the difficulty encountered in the typical MIS department stems from the existence of an "isolation" attitude on the part of many members of the department, including those who are members of management. Very little extra effort is made to reach out to those in other departments in order to better understand their particular needs and problems.

The manager of the MIS department should adopt a peripatetic approach to dealing with his department's clients. He should routinely visit the managers of other departments in order to achieve two goals. Through the use of direct visits, the manager can find out firsthand how well his department is doing in its effort to serve its clients. In addition, these visits will also improve the MIS image, in that they will help convince those in the client departments of the sincerity of the MIS management to improve the MIS service.

This issue of increased visibility is very important. Just the change involved in the MIS manager coming to the clients, rather than the usual approach where the clients always have to seek out the MIS manager, will have a salubrious effect on the MIS/client relationship. The more the feeling of openness the management of MIS can produce within the client areas, the better will be the ongoing effort.

There are several very effective methods which can be adapted by the MIS manager which will help ensure the improvement of relations between his department and the other departments within the organization. First, the manager should work to reduce the finger pointing which usually occurs when things go wrong. The idea should be to steer everyone involved away from attempting to fix the blame for whatever has happened, and to concentrate on solving the particular problem.

When everyone involved comes to accept the fact that the solution is much more important than who caused the problem, the climate between MIS and the clients will improve. As the climate improves, cooperation will increase and ultimately, other MIS/client difficulties will become less of a problem. There is an additional benefit; under this approach problems will be more quickly solved because the time being spent on accusations and denial will now be devoted to solving the problems.

The development of an "early warning system" should also be supported by MIS management. As an example, if the data center issues a production schedule (and if not, one should be in use) for batch processing, it will become apparent from time to time that particular production jobs will be late. When this schedule delay is realized by the data center staff, those clients who will be affected by the delay should be informed of both the delay and the anticipated new delivery time of the reports. A real irritant in the view of many MIS clients has to do with the expectation of the delivery of reports by a certain time, only to have the delivery time missed without any notice to the clients.

Effective use of a data center "early warning system" will help ease the client's concern about the delivery of their reports. It may not make the clients happy, but they will at least be able to better plan their work based upon the knowledge that the reports will be late. Because they are being informed in advance of problems, the MIS clients will come to see that MIS is indeed interested in their problems, and also that the MIS department, while it may be experiencing difficulty, is indeed on top of the problem.

The advent of on-line processing has produced a new element in the issue of the perception among MIS clients of the effectiveness of the MIS service. On-line processing, because it creates a more immediate atmosphere, requires an improved responsiveness on the part of MIS when difficulties arise. In the past, when most of the MIS orientation was to batch processing, many of the operational problems encountered by MIS could be hidden within the MIS department. On-line processing has opened up the MIS department environment to the MIS clients.

Because the clients are now more immediately aware of MIS difficulties (the CRTs are down), it is incumbent upon MIS to do a better job of keeping its clients informed. One approach which is being used to help improve the MIS/client climate is to install within the data center a "help desk" function. The idea is to provide a control point where MIS clients can obtain assistance with problems they may encounter, either with on-line processing or any other data center problems.

The "help desk" provides several features. It allows the clients to communicate with one, rather than several different people, for all their MIS operational problems. Also, in those organizations where clients can directly call the computer room and talk to the computer operators about problems, the service level of the data center will fall because the computer operators will be distracted. Often the computer operators are unable to resolve the problem anyway, and talking to them only causes delay and frustration.

The person who is assigned responsibility for the "help desk" function must have an awareness of the political aspects of the position. This is a service function and that orientation must pervade the work being done. The effectiveness of the work from a sales standpoint can go a long way toward burnishing the MIS image. As an example, MIS clients, particularly those with limited MIS experience, will call the help desk with rather basic problems, such as asserting that the system is inoperable, when in fact, they have neglected to turn on their CRT.

The manner in which problems of all types are handled by the person assigned to the MIS help desk must be a matter of concern to the management of the MIS department and care must be taken, not only in the selection of the people to do the job, but also in the ongoing monitoring of the work being done. Correctly staffed and managed, the help desk can provide an improved MIS environment, if it is not done correctly, the help desk will generate more harm than goodwill.

The idea of an MIS service level has merit. The MIS manager should give careful consideration to development of service level agreements with the MIS clients. What this entails is the establishment of criteria which can be used to judge, over time, the effectiveness of the MIS effort. That effectiveness can then be expressed in terms of service level, such as the achievement of a 98 percent service level. The value of such an approach is that it will show, over time, the relative performance of the MIS effort on an objective basis.

What are some of the items which should be included in the development of a service level agreement?

1. Compliance (as a percentage) with the MIS schedule. As an example, ninety-eight percent of all data center batch reports will be produced on time.
2. Maintenance of a hardware resource (both CPU and CRT) level above ninety-eight percent.
3. Consistent CRT response time of less than four seconds.
4. No more than three direct complaints to the senior MIS manager from clients in any quarter.
5. Completion of eighty-five percent of all MIS projects within the approved time and money budgets.

One of the underlying causes of difficulty between MIS and those it should attempt to serve can be found in the milieu of many MIS departments. Too many MIS departments operate in a mode of crisis management. This type of an environment obviously produces a deleterious effect on, not only the MIS clients, but also on members of the MIS department. Because very little attention is directed toward improvement of the operation or toward long-range planning, the situation simply becomes self-perpetuating, in that fires are consistently fought.

This, of course, results in undue tension within the MIS department, which in turn tends to spill over into the client areas. This is not only an unfortunate circumstance, it is also unnecessary! Appropriate management attention and control can remove the crisis environment within the MIS department, it does take time and effort, but it can (and it must) be done. As long as the MIS department operates in a crisis mode, the tension, both between MIS and its clients and within MIS, will only increase.

The "cultural" difficulties alluded to earlier can be seen within the MIS department itself. This situation might be described as a microcosm of that which occurs organizationwide. In many MIS departments there is a great deal of fractionalism. This is usually most apparent in the working relationships between the systems, programming, and the data center staffs.

The issue is often seen as an ongoing battle between these two groups over the allocation of MIS resources. Members of the systems and programming section will often stoutly maintain they are not being accorded sufficient resources in order to do their job. Conversely, the management of the data center will maintain that either more resource is not available (which may indeed be the case) or, that release of additional resources to the systems and programming group is not in the best interest of MIS, in terms of efficient use of the equipment. The latter position is often subjective.

This is a situation which should be resolved by the management of the MIS department. It is an unfortunate circumstance that many times the MIS management is more concerned with accommodating the needs of lower level clerks in client areas than with resolving internal MIS problems. Facing and resolving issues such as resource allocation within MIS can be difficult for MIS management, but they must not be ignored; they must be pursued and resolved.

The "cultural" problems found between MIS and the client departments is not restricted to the lower levels of the organization, it often affects senior management. To some extent, the problem is compounded at this level because in most cases, if it so chooses, senior management has the option to divorce itself from most MIS problems. Often the only time members of senior management become involved in the MIS function is through the development of some crisis which poses such a threat to the organization that it cannot be ignored.

In such a case it is usually the intention of senior management to identify the cause of the problems, to correct those problems, and move on to other things. While this does solve the immediate problem, senior management in such cases loses an opportunity to gain more in-depth knowledge of MIS.

When members of senior management are forced to take an active role in the solution of an MIS problem, often as the result of some situation which has taken on the aspect of a disaster, they see MIS and the interaction between MIS and its clients at their worst. Because the situation will usually have deteriorated to finger pointing, acrimony, and confusion, which will be further complicated by what will appear to senior management to be unintelligible jargon, those members of senior management who find themselves involved in such exercises will, in all likelihood, come away with their belief that MIS is a "necessary evil" reinforced.

Because of their reluctance to become involved in MIS concerns, and to do so only when there appears to be no other choice, members of senior management often come away more confused, and dismayed, about MIS than they were prior to their involvement. The often unfortunate result of such an encounter is the enforcement of the belief held by senior management that MIS may indeed be an almost unmanageable function, best left to the technicians to handle as best they can. Those members of senior management who do approach the subject with somewhat more fortitude, often find themselves involved in what appears to be an arcane world, one which often appears to bear little relationship to the particular business at hand.

The process is further compounded by senior management's difficulty to communicate with the members of the MIS team; this appears to be a world of strange technology, of black magic. Given these circumstances, it is not hard to understand the reluctance of members of senior management to immerse themselves in MIS. The pervasive nature of MIS, its growing importance to all areas of the organization means that, like it or not, senior management must work to overcome the tendency to let MIS go its own way. MIS management, at the same time, must also work to make the MIS function more understandable to senior management and work to put the MIS effort in terms which senior management finds easier to deal with.

However, cultural problems do not end with those outside the MIS department; there is considerable room for attention to these problems within the MIS department. Too many members of MIS, managers included, adopt a technical orientation; they attempt to impose technical solutions to all business problems, rather than to consider the business solutions and then attempt to find technical methods which can help solve the problem. Because of the technical orientation, the ability of members of MIS to effectively communicate with those outside the MIS department is impeded.

This problem can easily be seen in the continuing penchant of MIS employees to adopt the technical idiom, rather than business terms when talking to those outside the department. When someone from MIS attempts to explain a problem or solution to someone outside the department by discussing items such as "CPU seconds," "DASD," "head crashes," "CICS," "seek time," "channel contention," or "phase jitter" to name a few, the nontechnical person is certain to feel dismay. This may seem to be a rather ludicrous example, yet such conversations do indeed go on all the time.

The MIS management, which would like to obtain the trust and confidence of those the MIS department strives to serve, must be aware of and concerned with the issue of MIS credibility. Many MIS departments suffer from serious credibility problems, most of these problems have been generated over the years by MIS itself. Part of the problem is that too often what is promised by MIS is not delivered. Part of the problem is that MIS often attempts to do too much in too short a time.

While being a bit too ambitious and promising more than can be practically delivered can be annoying to the MIS clients, it can be resolved. What often causes a great deal of difficulty is the development of situations where MIS either refuses to admit difficulties, or attempts to make them appear to be less serious than they really are. No one likes to admit mistakes, but the constant manipulation of circumstances to attempt to place MIS in a better light than is factual, causes MIS clients difficulty with MIS over time.

The MIS manager who will accept responsibility by being willing to report lack of progress in a factual manner, who is willing to own up to MIS mistakes, and when they occur, MIS failures, will over time come to gain the respect of the MIS clients. Of course, too many failures will have an adverse effect on the career of the MIS manager, but otherwise good managers have been badly served by a propensity to be unwilling to admit to MIS failures or problems in a factual manner.

In spite of the preceding litany of problems, problems which are unfortunately more often the norm than the exception, much can be done to not only alleviate these problems but indeed to greatly improve the MIS/client relationship. The basic approach must be for members of MIS, led by the MIS management, to develop and use sound sales and marketing skills in their ongoing relationships with those who use the services of MIS, the MIS clients.

Surely any forward-looking MIS manager can discern that, given the coming changes in technology and technique, the MIS clients will increasingly become more sophisticated about the practice of information processing and will also become to an increasing degree, masters of their own information processing fate. It only follows then, that those MIS managers who see the advantages in taking the lead in helping the MIS clients better understand the MIS function, and who work to improve the MIS/client climate, will come out ahead.

Does this imply then that the successful MIS manager of the future will have to become a gregarious backslapper? No! It does mean, however, that the MIS manager, and at least the key members of the MIS staff, must build and maintain an improved rapport with the members of other departments within the organization. This effort to improve the rapport must be carried on at all levels. The key members of MIS must work hard to both convince and demonstrate to these clients that MIS wants to help them do their work in a more productive manner.

This improved sales/marketing approach to the improvement of the MIS/client relationship need not become a blatant sales campaign. Following the suggestions for improvement which have been outlined in prior sections of this chapter will certainly help in the effort. There is also another very effective approach which can be used which will provide MIS management an opportunity to bring the MIS story to a large segment of the client community, and which will also help demonstrate the MIS commitment to improved service to those clients.

The approach is to develop a series of MIS presentations. These presentations should be viewed by MIS management as both an opportunity to increase the clients awareness of the potential of the technology and also to carry forward the message of the scope and complexity of the organization's MIS function. It is interesting to discover as these presentations develop, how little knowledge and how many misconceptions exist about the MIS effort.

These presentations can be an excellent vehicle to explain some of the jargon used by members of MIS and which is found to be so confusing and annoying to those outside the MIS department. As the MIS acronyms are used in the presentations they should be explained. This will take some time, and it may be boring for those in attendance with an MIS background, but the effort will be appreciated and prove helpful to those without such a background.

While these presentations should be structured so as to inform the nonMIS participants, they should not adopt a tone which tends to "talk down" to those in attendance. If that happens, the effect of the sessions will be negative and the probably already poor public relations aspect of MIS will only be worsened.

What might such presentations include? To begin, there should be an overview of the MIS operational effort, the hardware used, the services rendered, and the number of operational programs and systems would be of interest. There should also be information about the MIS project development process, how do projects originate, how are they approved, developed, controlled, and implemented? What are some of the typical MIS concerns (the MIS/client relationship should be part of this presentation); how can they be improved? What about MIS long-range planning; what about the MIS effort (if any) to address the issue of contingency planning? The subject of future developments within MIS, relative to the changes in technology, and how those technical changes will impact the organization would be an excellent topic.

The purpose is to provide opportunities to share the concerns, the complexity, and the excitement of the MIS function with the MIS clients. The more these clients understand about the MIS process, the more empathy they will develop for the MIS employees. As they begin to appreciate the pressures faced by MIS, and the value of the work being done, not to mention the real potential in the MIS function, the relationship between MIS and all its clients will improve.

Just because many MIS/client relationships have been poor for a considerable time, there is no reason why those relationships cannot be improved. It is in the best interest, not only of MIS and its clients, but of the entire organization, to work hard to improve the environment. The game here is clearly worth the candle!

CHAPTER III
The Automated Office

The term, the Automated Office, is being used with increasing frequency throughout the business world. It is almost impossible to read any of the business periodicals without finding articles, or at least references, to the subject. The effort to increase the use of automation outside the more traditional MIS areas of the organization is growing at a rapid pace. The increasing practicability of applying the concepts of automation to these areas, coupled with the continuing declining costs associated with automation in all forms means not only that the growth will continue, but that the momentum to increase the uses of such automation will become increasingly rapid.

While efforts to increase the use of automation outside the boundaries of MIS are not only desirable but in fact necessary, there are any number of issues which, if the process is to be successful and if its true potential is to be realized, must be accorded appropriate attention. Failure to recognize the existence of these issues and to take action to bring them under control will mean that much of the difficulty encountered with MIS over the past twenty years is likely to recur as the automation of these office functions moves ahead.

There are currently any number of benefits to office automation, and as the technology grows, those benefits are certain to increase. The functions and capabilities available in the hardware and software offer very attractive opportunities for productivity increases.

Not only are tangible increases in productivity the norm, they are being realized in many instances at overall costs which are less, sometimes dramatically less, than current costs. Clearly this is a significant item. And it becomes more significant when one considers the fact that while the expenses associated with people (salaries and benefits) continue to rise, the hardware and software expenses, if for no other reason than that of increased competition, will continue to decline. Therefore, office automation does indeed offer a practical method to "do more for less."

Consideration of the history of investment by organizations in technology which will improve the productivity of office workers shows that, compared to other areas of business, very little money per worker has been invested. This may be due in part to the unavailability of suitable technology, or perhaps it is a result of well-known MIS problems which may have discouraged experimentation in these areas, in any case this now must change.

While the benefits can be substantial, as is the case with all considerations of the uses of technology, unless careful thought and planning are devoted to the management and control of office automation, the results achieved will be less than what has been expected and less than what should be expected. It is of great importance that sufficient consideration be given to the issues which surround the subject of office automation in order that, once installed, the process will be as successful as possible.

This is not meant to imply the development of a plan which will remove all risk taking in the office automation process. As has been the case with the development of the data processing function, there are bound to be mistakes and some failures; it is important that the approach taken minimizes the risk wherever possible. The office automation issue affords many organizations the opportunity to "do it right the first time." Drawing on the lessons learned with MIS and using those lessons in a constructive manner will produce much greater success with much less trauma.

The timing in many organizations concerning the introduction of office automation now presents real opportunity. There are two reasons. First, the effort is just beginning in many organizations, so it can indeed be started and carried on correctly. Second, because of the similarity to the MIS process, that is the use of technology (albeit on a less complex scale) to overcome problems, much of the experiences gained through years of trial and error effort in attempting to improve the MIS function can be transferred to office automation. The potential to do it right the first time is there, whether those involved will prove to be astute enough to take advantage of this circumstance remains to be seen.

It would be quite appropriate for whomever is charged with the responsibility for the office automation function to, as a preliminary step, review the growth of the organization's MIS function. In doing this, attention should be given to the identification of those areas where things have gone less than well. Once these areas have been identified, they should be carefully examined to ascertain the causes of the problems. Questions should be posed about the specifics of the problems and their causes. Was the planning poorly done? Did communications fail? Was inappropriate technology selected and installed? Were vendors allowed too much control? Was there sufficient senior management involvement?

Just as there are no unique MIS problems, it is also correct that, aside from the specific functions, there is very little difference between the work being done in MIS and the work which will be accomplished under the aspects of the office automation function. While, in all likelihood, managers with particular political ground to defend will insist that there are vast differences between the two, that is really a spurious argument. Office automation is simply one more application of the use of technology to improve the organization; considerable time and energy can be saved if this fact is recognized at the onset and people move to more important considerations.

In addition to the normal difficulties one would expect to find in the introduction of this new technology into new areas of the organization, it should also be anticipated that there will be considerable political infighting along the way. Perhaps not all the political difficulty can be avoided; however, with appropriate effort and management, much of it can, in fact should, be avoided.

Prior to giving in to the euphoria of moving to the "automated office," appropriate consideration should be given to some of those areas where conflict is likely to arise and then to develop practical solutions to the resolution of those problems. Some of the probable issues are:

- Long-Range Planning
- Excessive Hardware/Software Expense
- Political/Territorial Conflicts
- Personal Issues
- Obsolescence
- Incompatibility of Hardware and Software

A chronic problem in many MIS departments has been the failure to develop and then enact long-range plans. Too often forces external to the MIS department have been allowed to shape the course of MIS and have created a general acceptance of operating in a crisis mode as a normal way of MIS life. In those organizations where an attempt has been made to carry out long-range planning, it is often the case that either the plan does not pertain to the business strategy of the organization, or it has been too rigid.

The issue of long-range planning is the same for office automation as for MIS. Unless an organizational strategy is formulated which the office automation plan can be built around, the problems encountered with office automation in the future will be greater than necessary. Of course, the office automation plan must also be developed with at least a consideration of the current and future plans for the MIS effort. There must be sufficient linkage between these functions to assure appropriate coordination and cooperation.

The problem is that in the absence of a sound office automation plan, the uses of the technology may well prove to be less than desirable. The goal must be to key all office automation planning to the organization's overall strategy, rather than to allow automation to simply evolve in some haphazard manner. A very serious problem facing many MIS departments today is to come to the realization that much of what has been done in the MIS department has been done in an unplanned, uncoordinated manner, that there is little real integration and that now much of what has been done needs to be redone. Careful, comprehensive planning with regard to the subject of office automation can help avoid such a situation in the office automation areas.

As an example, it would appear to be rather clear that the issue of compatibility between various hardware and software components, even within the same vendor offerings, is one which should not be ignored. However, unless there is some type of umbrella strategy in place with appropriate controls, the time will very likely come when the issue of incompatibility will become a very real, and perhaps a very expensive, issue.

This is already occurring in a number of organizations. The ability of the various department managers to select and install whatever type of automated equipment they desire is causing considerable consternation at high levels of organization as it becomes apparent that chaos is occurring. To a large extent, this is a result of the activity of vendor representatives being able to convince managers who are technically naive that, if these managers even think to ask the question, everything can be tied together. Often this is either incorrect, or can only be accomplished at considerable expense and technical frustration.

What happens when, after several years of fragmented installation of various types of office automation equipment, it is decided that everything should be tied together through some type of networking arrangement in order to reduce expense and to gain improved control of the office automation functions? What will then occur will be a costly venture to redress the problems which will have been generated through the lack of appropriate planning. Ultimately, what may occur, is the removal of much of the currently installed hardware and software in order to move to an environment which will provide the required compatibility.

This will prove to be not only a costly, but also an extremely frustrating experience for everyone involved. It may require additional training, on top of an already sizable investment in training for the currently installed software and hardware, for many of those who will use the new equipment. Such changes will certainly cause morale problems. Such a change may also bring about the requirement to convert the data which has been developed on the various incompatible office automation systems in use.

There should be no mistake; regardless of what the vendor representatives may claim, the conversion of data from one system to another format may prove to be a very long and a very frustrating experience. The problem may be, given certain circumstances, that there will not be any option except to go through the conversion process. A long-range plan, linked to an office automation strategy with appropriate policies in place, can forestall many of the problems associated with such a situation.

The imposition of a long-range office automation plan will also help assure that sound projects are initiated and that they are followed through to completion. All effort undertaken in the name of office automation can be examined against the overall plan; the results of these efforts can then be tracked against the plan to determine if the project has indeed been completed and if the results have been effective.

One of the problems inherent in the piecemeal installation of office automation is that often a piece of equipment is brought in for one purpose, such as word processing, and the other benefits of the system, as an example the ability to carry out accounting functions, are not realized. The increasing versatility of the equipment being installed makes its limited use a very costly venture. If the capability of the equipment is correctly understood, and if the department is correctly organized, much more can be accomplished with the same investment in equipment than may at first be realized.

The issue of political/territorial concerns is one which has not usually been a problem in the evolution of the MIS function within the organization. The complexity of the MIS function, the requirement to possess special knowledge, and the fact that the MIS effort has typically been restricted to a central location, have mitigated much of the problem about who should control equipment and about the people who should be involved in the MIS effort. The answer has generally been that the entire effort was within the purview of MIS management.

Now, with the advent of equipment which greatly simplifies much of what has always been the sole responsibility of MIS, coupled with the portability of hardware which no longer requires a special environment, and with the aggressive effort on the part of vendors to sell the equipment and software outside the MIS department, the territorial battle lines have been drawn.

The MIS manager, facing a loss of control and prestige, will usually begin an effort to protect his domain. This often takes the shape of an attempt to restrict the introduction of all equipment which is not approved by MIS management. Managers of other departments, encouraged by the vendors, and sensing the ease with which they will be able to automate some of their functions, will begin to work to circumvent the MIS department. What happens is that instead of working together to help move the organization ahead, time and energy will be expended in the really unproductive process of battling for territory.

The development of this rather common phenomenon is not entirely due to machinations on the part of the nonMIS managers and the vendors, often MIS management must share the blame. In fact, in many instances MIS managers have encouraged, if not forced, such circumstances to occur. Much of the progress being made in the introduction of office automation has occurred as a result of MIS departments being unwilling to respond to the requests of other departments for assistance.

This effort on the part of nonMIS management to go their own way with office automation is not a particularly bad situation; it can and often does work to drive the organization ahead. Rather than wait, or deal with recalcitrant MIS management, these managers simply go ahead on their own. While the long-term results of such effort may be undesirable, the short-term result is that the job does get done.

This issue of territorial control should not be ignored; it must be addressed and resolved. The specific approach to the resolution of the problem will of course be different within particular organizations. This will depend upon the determination within the organization of that which is best, both with regard to the organizational climate, and also with regard to the demonstrated skills of the various managers involved. As an example, while the MIS manager may be able to produce a quite plausible case for all office automation being placed under the control of MIS, perhaps citing issues such as expense savings, technological expertise, and comprehensive knowledge of vendor methods, the current MIS function may be in such a state of disrepair that any attempt to assume additional responsibility would be tantamount to folly.

Regardless of which department ultimately obtains control of the office automation function, it should be a centralized control. This does not mean that the equipment should all be centrally located as is the case with the typical typing pool today, but that the selection, placement, and overall control of that equipment should be centralized in one department.

Perhaps the function should be defined as being outside the purview of the current MIS administrative function and should be placed, either in the office administration function or as a separate office administration function. Again, the particular political climate and perceived competence of the potential managers should be the compelling factors in the final decision. The important point to keep in mind is to work to avoid allowing the function to become fragmented.

In any event, the scope of the office automation implementation effort must, as a first step, be clearly defined. The process which will lead to this definition should include a series of questions. Does office automation include MIS? Should it be a subset of MIS? Should it be a separate function? Does office automation include telecommunications, if so does it include both voice and data? The subject of telecommunications is an increasingly important aspect of both office automation and MIS; its importance must not be overlooked.

It should be understood that the subject of office automation is rather more large and complex than may at first be realized. It is not, as is often believed, and encouraged by vendors, a simple matter of replacing typewriters with word processing equipment. In fact, it is safe to speculate that the truly single function word processing system is probably entering a phase out condition. Much of the newly introduced equipment offers very good word processing capability as one factor in a larger range of computerized functions. This fact should be kept in mind as one considers the selection of equipment. Failure to recognize the scope and complexity of the subject and to develop a comprehensive plan which will help set the correct course for the future is a mistake.

This is a mistake which has been made in many organizations, and will continue to be made! In order to address these issues, the development of an Office Automation Committee which has as its responsibility the review of requests for equipment, the development of policies, and a mandate to provide direction and control with regard to the issues of office automation should be considered. The function of this group will be similar to that of an MIS Steering Committee; indeed it would be appropriate to set up this group as a subset of the Steering Committee. As is the case with the MIS Steering Committee, this group can provide a very effective method of avoiding many of the problems encountered with office automation when everyone is allowed to go their own way.

Because of the myriad personnel problems which are a normal part of the process of introducing office automation, the Office Automation Committee should include a representative of the personnel department. Because the introduction of office automation usually is in areas which have not been affected by any type of automation in the past, as an example, in the typing pool; the initial impact on employees in these areas is often negative.

Given the unease in these departments which are being affected by automation for the first time, it will usually not take long for rumors to

CHAPTER III

begin to circulate. The primary concern is, of course, the fear that the introduction of the equipment means a loss of jobs. This may in fact be the case; if it is, so be it. The presence of someone from the personnel department should help bring some sensitivity to the issue. This person should be able to suggest ways to mitigate the problem. If, indeed, the purpose is the reduction of personnel, that fact should be admitted to and dealt with; it should not be covered up.

While it is not always recognized, the advances in technology are rapidly creating opportunities to eliminate the traditional Data Entry sections found in many organizations. The available hardware and software allow the clients within the departments to enter their own data directly to the mainframe. This reduces cost and duplication of effort, because the input does not have to be coded one place and keyed somewhere else, and it provides increased flexibility with regard to constraints of the MIS production schedules.

Because this can and should be done, the personnel problems which will be generated by such an action must be handled in a fashion which will not destroy morale, and which will achieve a positive impact with regard to the entire process. If the organization will take the time to develop a plan for the transfer of the data entry work from the data entry section to the clients, if that plan is explained to all concerned, and if the elimination of the data entry section is accomplished through attrition, and if those who remain in data entry are provided opportunities to assume jobs elsewhere in the organization (perhaps as data entry people in the client departments) much of the anguish and fear associated with the process can be reduced.

In all instances where office automation is introduced, whether to eliminate existing functions, to improve existing functions, or to enter into new processes, if appropriate consideration of employees' feelings and a well-planned sales effort are carried out, much of the trauma can be mitigated. If office automation is introduced in a cavalier fashion, with little apparent regard for those it will affect, the effort will be much more difficult and much less successful.

An additional personnel problem, at all levels of the organization when automated functions are being introduced, is that of overcoming the reluctance to accept change. People, at all levels of the organization not just those at the clerical level, have a fear of appearing foolish. Because they are not familiar with the equipment and because it all seems so complex, it is often difficult to get people to attempt to learn the new processes. In order to be successful, this factor must be considered and appropriate care exercised to make certain people are made comfortable as they begin to learn these new functions.

This introduction of office automation into new areas of the organization must be handled very carefully. There is no assurance that the installation of the office automation equipment will be successful. The key to the success, of course, lies with the acceptance and use of the equipment by those who must use it in their normal work. If this fact is ignored, and if these employees feel that the equipment is being forced upon them, the task will not only become much more difficult, it will be more likely to fail. This is unfortunate, because once a failure has been encountered, the effort required to overcome the bad publicity will be great.

The ease with which the office automation introduction is made, and its eventual success depends upon the attitude of those who use it. If several people in a department refuse to accept the equipment, the process will be very difficult. This is the case because usually the most serious problem found when installing the equipment is dealing with the fear of those to whom it is new. Great care should be taken to assure that the most practical "comfort level" has been achieved.

The selection of those who will install the office automation equipment and help train those who will use it is important. Technical knowledge and skills are not as important here as a patient attitude, coupled with a strong desire to help people learn. The higher quality software available today provides a great deal of programmed instruction which can make learning the use of the equipment on an independent basis very practical. In this environment, all that is required is someone with experience to help the student get started, to answer questions when necessary, and to provide encouragement.

Unless the organization is exceedingly small, it will become apparent, often after much frustration, that a set of office automation policies are required. It makes good sense to recognize this fact at the onset and to work to develop those policies prior to their actual need. In the absence of a set of policies, and the facility to enforce those policies, the issues of duplication of effort and data, of increased hardware and personnel costs, and general lack of sound direction will become real problems as time goes on.

One example of the requirement for a set of office automation policies can be seen in an examination of the issue of centralization or distribution of the function. Should all office automation be done on the MIS department hardware; should it all be done on "stand alone" hardware in the various departments; or, should there be some combination of the two? Questions of costs, of personnel, and of the political realities must be considered and a reasonable judgment made based upon the facts, with an appropriate policy in place (and enforced) which will support that decision.

This is another example of the myriad options open to those who must deal with the several issues of automation. Some framework must be in place which will work to assure that the time and money spent to automate office functions is practical, and that the results are in line with the goals and desires of senior management. What is to be avoided is to find that the course taken in automating these functions has been taken by default.

These policies need not be complex or lengthy. They should address whatever issues appear to be of concern within the organization. Their purpose is to outline that which can, and that which cannot be done, and who has responsibility for specific areas of office automation. Of course, policies do not, by themselves, assure that all will go well. Without some type of audit, there is no assurance that they will be followed. However, they do provide a basis for control and a tool to redress breaches of policy when they occur.

This question of who should control what aspect of the office automation function can be difficult to resolve. One reason for the development of separate responsibilities for various aspects of office automation is an attempt to mitigate some of the political problems which arise over the questions of authority and control of the particular functions. The concern of individual managers is understandable. However, awarding various sections a "piece of the action," may cause less political trauma within the organization; yet it will, in all likelihood, increase costs and the overall problems of control.

The issue of duplication of data, an issue which has now been recognized as a critical problem within MIS departments, will, unless it is controlled at an early stage, grow into a major problem in the office automation function. If everyone is allowed to go their own way without regard for the consequences of work being done or the data being generated, the same general types of data will be generated in several different areas of the organization for separate functions. While in practice it may not be feasible, or practical, where possible all data should be generated from one source. Copies of that data should then be made available to those who have a need to use the data in order to produce the information they require.

As an example, consider the rather straightforward issue of the organization's Customer Data Base. An insurance company might have a requirement for using the information about its insureds in a variety of ways. The claims department may want to obtain information about the claims history of a particular group of insureds. The sales department may want a listing of all insureds in a particular area in order to solicit increased business. The underwriting department may desire the same information produced by rating territory or by age group. The central files group may require the information in alphabetical order, or perhaps by policy number, or perhaps, by a cross index of alpha and number sequence.

If these and other needs are to be met, and if all areas are allowed to go their own way and build and maintain their own files on their own equipment, a great deal of unnecessary effort and redundant data will be generated. It will become difficult, probably impossible, to maintain this information so that it is always in syncopation with the other departments' customer master files. It is much better to centralize such information and to provide whatever is needed by a department from that central data base. This will assure uniformity and that all information used is the same at all times.

One of the past concerns was that the ability to link *microprocessors* to mainframe hardware was not a practical matter. There are currently at least limited software packages which will allow this linkage with some of the more popular *micro*s and the availability of that software is certain to grow as time goes on.

This means that an expanded role for microprocessors in the office automation effort in the context of being able to access existing organizational data bases is becoming a reality. This offers great benefits, in that one of the real difficulties inherent in the use of microprocessors, the requirement to enter large amounts of data, can now be overcome. The data is now accessible to these small machines, and therefore their capability is being enhanced.

There are several hardware issues which should not be overlooked. If it is determined that stand alone hardware is the most appropriate equipment for the automation of office functions, the questions of cost, capacity, functions, and obsolescence must be carefully considered. The environment each piece of equipment is to be put into and the work to be done should be understood in order that appropriate choices within the context of the above issues can be made.

How much should be spent on the stand alone equipment will often be determined by the functions to be performed. As an example, if word processing is the only function to be handled, equipment which can perform more sophisticated processes in addition to word processing may not be worth the expense. Before that decision is made however, it should be established that something more than word processing will not become a requirement throughout the probable life of the equipment. As a practical matter, as has already been stated, the purchase of single function word processing equipment should be avoided.

The capacity of the equipment to be installed must also be given careful consideration. In so far as practical, an attempt should be made to predict the growth of the system requirements over the anticipated life of the equipment. The equipment selected should be large enough to accommodate this growth, and should in fact be larger, because it is very likely that the actual growth will be larger than has been anticipated. Many organizations have discovered, to their dismay, that the equipment they have installed has not been large enough to accommodate the growing demand.

If the equipment is leased, provision should be made to expand the equipment or to move to larger equipment as required through the term of the lease. If purchased, and capacity is exceeded, it is unlikely that any remedy, other than purchasing a new system will be an appropriate answer. Care must be exercised with regard to the purchase of office automation equipment. The technology changes so rapidly, that obsolescence occurs very rapidly. This means that the residual value of the equipment in terms of applying its value to the purchase of new equipment is usually very small.

In order to obtain some sense of security when attempting to obtain an idea of the likely capacity needs of the office automation equipment, it would appear to be prudent, after careful investigation of the growth requirements over the anticipated life of the equipment, to double the figure arrived at and use that figure as the basis for determining growth needs. It is better to come to the end of the equipment life cycle with a bit of excess capacity than to exceed that capacity halfway through the life cycle.

The general question of hardware and software obsolescence is one which must be carefully considered. The equipment and the software will change rapidly, both in function and in price. It can be taken as an axiom that the functions will always improve and that cost, at least in relation to these improved functions, will always drop. Given that circumstance, it is clear that today's leading edge office automation hardware and software will, in all likelihood, become obsolete in a very short time. Therefore, it behooves those charged with selecting the hardware to make the best possible choices with regard to the technology.

While the fact of obsolescence must simply be accepted, if the office automation planning has been well-done, the equipment selected, provided the time frame covered is not excessive (probably not more than three years), should be quite satisfactory. Again, any statements from the vendors about long-range upgradability should be treated with skepticism. These statements may be quite correct, yet the buyer must beware.

The issue of compatibility between various makes of hardware and software must not be ignored. While the issue is being given increasing attention by the various vendors and while progress is being made, there is still a considerable way to go in order to resolve the issue. When installing new office automation hardware and software, even if other items from that particular vendor are installed, compatibility must not be ignored.

Assurances from the vendor that compatibility is a minor problem, one which once the equipment is installed can be easily rectified, should be critically considered. What may be presented as a small concern prior to the sale can indeed become a major issue after installation of the hardware/software. If there is any doubt whatsoever in this area, all representations should be covered and supported as a binding aspect of the purchase contract. The vendor's agreement or reluctance to put his claims in writing should be a key to the ease of accomplishing compatibility.

No one has a crystal ball when it comes to the life span of office automation equipment or to the requirements for compatibility in the future. As is the case with any other aspect of information processing, waiting will only delay the advantages to be gained from the use of this advanced technology. Careful, thorough investigation should be carried on, the most appropriate selection made based upon the facts, and management should then move on to other concerns.

The propensity to delay, to wait for the forthcoming dramatic new announcement, should be avoided. With office automation, as with all information processing functions, most decisions, examined later on, in the light of new developments will be open to criticism. Rather than attempt to protect themselves later on through a process of delay, management has a responsibility to select the currently best available solution and go with that solution. Progress in these areas is not made by the timid; those who spend too much time "looking over their shoulders" do their organizations and themselves a disservice.

CHAPTER IV
Preparing for a Data Processing Disaster

The universal reliance upon computers within business organizations carries with it the equally universal potential for disaster: The potential for the occurrence of an organizational calamity lurks within the confines of every organization's computer room. The origin of this calamity has nothing to do with those more commonly recognized scenarios of computer generated difficulties. For example, difficulties such as those which arise from such occurrences as computer programs which do not perform correctly, data processing systems which deliver less (often substantially less) than they were originally designed to deliver, and which, in the bargain, may be brought into production much later than had been originally promised. These difficulties have nothing to do with computer operational problems which may generate horrors such as the issuance of erroneous Customer Invoices, the destruction of Accounts Receivable computer files, or the development of incorrect factory production schedules.

Problems of that type, while always annoying, often frustrating, and on occasion very serious, do not represent the ultimate data processing disaster. The ultimate disaster, at least within the confines of the data processing function and its relation to the rest of the organization, is represented by the loss of the availability of an organization's computers.

While it is a widely held, albeit totally incorrect, belief of many members of senior management that they are able to exercise only minimal control over their organization's data processing function, protection from a disaster of the magnitude inherent in the physical loss of the computer can be managed by nontechnical people. It may indeed be most appropriate that the responsibility be given to someone outside the data processing department. The question, "What happens to the organization if we lose the computer?" is one which must receive increased senior management attention.

It is entirely appropriate to equate the loss of those spinning tape and disk drives, the flashing Cathrode Ray Tubes (CRTs), and the ubiquitous (even though highly undesirable) reams of computer printout with a "going out of business" scenario. Data Processing has become such an integral part of many organizations that it has, like it or not, become inseparable from the total business. In some organizations, it is impossible to determine where the computer ends and the business begins. Whether this was planned, whether or not it is considered desirable, the fact remains, the computer has indeed become a significant part of the organization.

Statements to the effect that the computer is inseparable from the organization are sometimes met with skepticism by members of senior management. However, even a cursory examination of those organizational functions which would be disrupted, if not entirely lost, within a given organization in the event of the loss of a viable data processing function will demonstrate the degree, often unrealized by senior management, of organizational dependence upon the computer.

The typical organization will not only currently have a number, often a large number, of critical systems (critical in the sense of being absolutely essential to the continued operation of the business) being processed on the computer; but will, in all likelihood, possess a large backlog of new or revised systems waiting to be developed and implemented. This demonstrates not only the current vulnerability of the organization with regard to the loss of the computer, but also that the passage of time will simply exacerbate that vulnerability. The current thrust, almost irrespective of the perceived quality of the current data processing function, in all organizations is for more, not less, computerization.

As organizations continue the march toward, and as they become increasingly involved with, the establishment of "on-line," "real time," "data base," and "teleprocessing" functions (and like it or not, competitive pressure, if nothing else, will continue these trends at a rapid pace), the more critical becomes the requirement to continue that processing, regardless of the status of the in-house data processing facility. Loss of the computer must not be allowed to translate to loss of the organization, yet that is precisely the case in a large number of organizations today.

This issue of loss of the computer facility is rather more complex than merely, "either we have the computer, or we don't." A loss of less than the total system can produce havoc. Absolute destruction of the computer facility can, without appropriate precautions, represent complete disaster. Unavailability of access to the computer for several days can also represent a disaster, albeit of somewhat less magnitude.

CONTINGENCY PLANNING

Two examples of the impact of sound contingency planning, or the lack of such planning, will help illustrate the vulnerability of organizations to such occurrences which are beyond their direct control. It should be kept in mind that while in one instance the physical damage was substantial; the actual damage, compared to the potential damage to the ongoing operation, was in both cases minimal.

The first example is that of a large retailer with a complex data center function. This organization was without an extant disaster plan, although some consideration had been given to the need to develop a plan.

As a result of what was later determined to be a rather minor data processing hardware failure, a large-scale computer in the organization's data center was inoperable for several days. It should be understood that in this instance, no physical damage had been done to the data center itself; from all outward appearances, everything was fine. A great deal of confusion ensued in the attempt to locate a site where the organization's data processing could be carried on. Although such a site was found, all efforts to resume processing at that location were unsuccessful.

While this particular incident could not be considered serious within the context of disaster planning, that is the data center had not been harmed in any way and the required backup data files were available for offsite processing, the result was expensive. This rather minor disruption, which put the data center out of operation for several days, incurred expenses of $750,000.00 in lost computer processing production, and $75,000.00 spent for various recovery elements which proved to be ineffective.

Conversely, an example of the ability to overcome a severe disaster as a result of sound contingency planning and testing can be seen in the case of a medium-sized, publicly owned financial services organization whose data center and its equipment were completely destroyed. This data center is located in the Midwest; the disaster occurred during the extremely cold winter of 1981. The data center in a subterranean location of a major office building was flooded by the bursting of a thirty-inch water main which was caused by the severe weather.

This flooding was described as a "tidal wave followed by a river of water," which poured down a one-hundred foot corridor and into the computer room. After the initial panic subsided and it was determined that no employees were injured, the on-site staff began to immediately implement the disaster plan. Fortunately, the company had a strong contingency plan, which included a contract with a backup site facility.

As a result, the batch computer systems were running on the backup site equipment within twelve hours of the occurrence of the flood. An assessment of the damage at the original site revealed the equipment was beyond repair. Within thirty-six hours of the occurrence of the flood, the organization's on-line systems were also operational at the backup site.

The original data center was restored in less than two weeks, new equipment was installed, and for the next two weeks jobs were processed in parallel at both sites to check out the new equipment. The happy ending in this case is, in the face of a far greater loss, service to customers was not disturbed and because of insurance, the actual expense in the end was minor.

There are any number of organizations today, and the list grows rapidly, which simply cannot tolerate the loss of their operational data processing functions for a period as short as several days. Others, because of their dependence upon on-line, real time processing, face serious difficulty with the loss of a day, or, in some instances, even several hours of processing time. Anyone who has attempted to transact business at a teller's window in a bank when the computer is "down" has firsthand knowledge of the problems presented with the loss of a real time processing system. Further consideration of the magnitude of the difficulties posed by the loss of the computer in a typical organization will demonstrate the serious implications of that loss.

Consider, as an example, an organization, one not terribly sophisticated, which depends on an on-line data processing system. This particular system is used to accept and process sales orders from the field. As the orders are entered, the system uses that data to update and adjust other information systems within the organization. This might include systems such as materials purchases, finished goods inventories, sales histories, accounts payable, general ledger, and customer invoices. It would be safe to assume that such a system would have sufficient sophistication to detect incorrect orders as they enter the system, hold those erroneous orders for correction, and to produce invoices for all orders which are determined to be error free.

Because of its reliance upon such a system, what is the effect on the total organization, not simply the data processing operation, should access to these data processing systems be lost for several days, a week, a month, forever? Unfortunately, many organizations are, despite an advanced degree of data processing sophistication, ill-prepared to cope with a loss of their data processing capabilities for as little as several days, not to mention any longer period of time. However, a catastrophe within the computer room, a fire, building collapse, or the malicious action of persons outside (or inside) the organization, can render the data processing capability of an organization useless for weeks or longer.

Of course, some industries are far more dependent upon their data processing functions than others. Therefore, the loss of the data processing function will be more serious in some organizations than in others. Organizations such as airlines, financial concerns, or police networks are clearly more vulnerable to the loss of the computer than others. However, the proliferation of data processing and the increasing reliance on on-line, real time processing in industries and organizations of all sizes makes the issue of sound data processing contingency planning crucial. Size has nothing to do with need.

In far too many organizations, the typical situation is that little, often no, effective data processing contingency planning has been carried on. Clearly, effective data processing contingency planning and response to emergency situations cannot be carried out on a retroactive basis. Solid, effective work in this area must be done, and must be tested prior to the arrival of the need.

Given the scope of the data processing effort being carried on in the preceding example, it is not at all difficult to imagine the absolute chaos the organization will encounter if it is forced to deal with the loss of its computer. The degree of that chaos will be increased in direct proportion to the lack, or weakness, of a data processing contingency plan. The loss of the computer facility will, even given the existence of a sound, well-tested data processing contingency plan, place severe strain on everyone in the organization. The absence of such a plan, or attempting to rely upon a partial plan, assures a real disaster.

There are two distinct aspects to a sound contingency plan. The disaster plan covers the overall approach to the recovery of the data processing function in the event of its loss, regardless of its cause. As a subset of the disaster plan, a series of procedures must be developed which cover every aspect of the approach to be implemented in the event of a disaster. These sections of the disaster plan must provide sufficient detail to assure that the plan, if it must be enacted, will function properly.

Obviously, the loss of the computer affects much more than just the data processing function. Given the existence of a sound, regularly tested contingency plan, an organization operating at even a low level of sophistication may require several working days to resume that which might be considered something close to a normal level of its processing function. The reaction time and the complex logistics involved in the relocation of the data processing operation will necessitate this requirement, even with a strong data processing contingency plan. Those organizations with weak contingency plans, the majority might, with luck, resume operation in six or eight working days, provided a great deal of effort is expended, and good luck is involved.

Where data processing is involved, the loss of eight working days processing is, in itself, a formidable matter. Being faced with eight days time to resume something akin to normal operation means that those eight lost days must somehow be regained. Completing that effort will, in itself, be a large task. It would not be unreasonable to speculate that some, perhaps all, of that eight days' business would be lost. In the preceding example, that would amount to four million dollars of gross income. In a medium-size installation, a strong effective plan can be designed, installed, and tested for less than $25,000.00, and maintained on an annual basis for less than $35,000.00 per year.

In those organizations where no contingency plan exists, the loss of eight days' business could very well be considered a small price to pay when balanced against the very likely probability that, without a plan, the organization is not going to reopen its doors. The lack of strong, effective, thoroughly tested, and regularly updated data processing contingency planning, does indeed represent a "going out of business" scenario!

If the need for an awareness of the potential of a data processing disaster, and the subsequent construction of a sound contingency plan is so obvious, the appropriate question to ask would appear to be, "Why is so little being done; why is so little attention being paid to this subject?" There are several reasons. Unfortunately, in far too many organizations, awareness of the total impact of a data processing disaster does not usually become apparent to members of senior management unless a disaster, or a near disaster, occurs. The issue may be raised in audit reports. In fact, the subject is becoming an increasing concern of auditors. However, it is usually the case that either senior management overlooks the issue when raised in an audit, or assumes that the problem is being addressed in the data processing department. After all, doesn't data processing contingency planning have something to do with data processing?

This assumption, that members of the data processing staff are addressing this problem is, much more often than not, false. The subject of data processing contingency planning is not one which will usually be addressed with any degree of fervor by those directly responsible for the data processing function.

There are several reasons why this is the case; reasons which, in the view of the typical data processing manager, always appear to be quite plausible. Usually the data processing manager is preoccupied with what he considers to be far more important issues. These are issues of some immediacy, such as maintaining the work flow through his department, dealing with what appear to be interminable crises (crises which are a result, more often than not, of poor data processing management), and dealing with the complaints of those who require his services. Given this situation, the manager will contend he has insufficient time to provide adequate attention to a subject as important as long-range planning; how can he be expected to devote time to something as mundane as data processing contingency planning?

The issue of funding will also be raised as a reason for not instituting an effective data processing contingency plan. While this planning does require an expenditure to design, install, and maintain, the total expense when balanced against either the data processing department budget, or the probable expense which will be incurred in the event of a disaster and the lack of an effective plan, is small indeed.

These concerns, lack of time and funds, while they do have some merit, must not be allowed to become deterrents to the implementation of a strong contingency plan. These issues are often raised, yet they are often a screen for that which is, in many instances, the real reason for lack of action on the part of the data processing staff with regard to contingency planning. It is important to realize that data processing contingency planning is, unfortunately, a rather routine, unexciting process. Those directly responsible for the organization's data processing functions will usually turn their attention to those subjects which they view as challenging, or having a "state of the art" connotation. Data processing contingency planning definitely does not fit that criteria.

In addition, there is also the quite normal feeling that the loss of the data processing facility is something that always happens to someone else. This idea that such things "always happen to the other fellow" constitutes a very high risk gamble. Unfortunately, this gamble is being taken at a rather low organizational level, often by those who do not stand to lose a great deal should that gamble be lost.

The demonstrated proclivity of data processors to align their loyalty to the data processing profession, rather than their current employer, is also a factor with regard to lack of interest in data processing contingency planning. Many people engaged in data processing would feel little, if any, compunction about expressing the feeling that, should disaster strike, other jobs with other organizations are always available.

These factors should raise several issues for any organization's senior management! A change of attitude on the part of senior management as it pertains to the data processing function must come about. This is beginning to happen as more people who possess an understanding and a working knowledge of the functions of data processing move to the senior levels of organizations. While it is still rather common for members of senior management to view the data processing function as, at best, a necessary evil, an item of burden, or overhead, the fact remains, the computer with its potential for either good or ill, has simply become too important to the total organization to continue to be ignored at the highest organizational levels.

Much of the difficulty related to data processing efforts can be traced to a lack of understanding, interest, and commitment to the subject on the part of senior management. A fear of the unknown, a lack of willingness to learn on the part of senior management has not rendered the work of the data processors any easier; it has also helped keep overall data processing results from being more meaningful in any number of organizations. Given those circumstances, it should not be surprising that senior management holds little awareness of the absolutely critical nature of strong, effective, data processing contingency planning.

Given such a situation, what can be done to make certain a sound, effective data processing contingency plan is instituted? First, the management of the data processing function must be required to produce a detailed report which covers the current status of the organization's data processing contingency planning. This will, in all likelihood, produce some rather interesting results. In many instances it will be found no plan of any kind exists. If there is a plan, the next question is, "What steps are being taken to test, and to regularly update, the plan?"

Should there be no plan, one must be developed on an immediate basis. Any data processing plan must, if it is to have any validity, address the following items:

The plan must be in writing. It must have been reviewed by an appropriate member of senior management, and must have been formally approved by that person.

The plan must detail, in very specific terms, the criteria which constitutes a disaster within the organization. This determination of those specific conditions, which will constitute a disaster for this particular organization, is important. Awareness of, and agreement to, those conditions by the organization's senior management is also important!

The implementation of the contingency plan will prove to be a complex and time consuming process. The time, effort, and coordination required to implement the plan, even a well-developed and maintained plan, will be significant. The process then should only begin in the event of an actual disaster.

It may be known to the employees in the data processing department, based upon factors such as: the processing being carried on, the quality of the offsite backup files, and the competency of the staff that a loss of as much as three concurrent days processing can be lost and subsequently recovered without the requirement to enact the contingency plan. This approach (do nothing until the lost processing time has, or will, exceed three days' work) may be quite appropriate from a data processing point of view. However, senior management may, for a variety of reasons, be they pragmatic, political, or philosophical, feel that any loss of processing time in excess of perhaps twelve hours, be considered unacceptable. If this is the case, an entirely different emphasis must be placed on the implementation of the contingency plan by the data processing department.

What must be avoided is either a rush to implement the plan when that is not required, or conversely, the adoption of a complacent attitude when something more urgent is required by senior management. Data processing management should propose a time frame for implementation, based upon their knowledge of the quality of both the data processing function and the data processing contingency plan. Senior management must fully understand what this means in terms of impact upon the total organization and agree to the proposed time frame. Heated discussion of the failure to implement the plan in twelve hours, three days after the loss of the data processing facility, due to the failure on the part of data processing management and senior management to have reached prior agreement on the topic is neither productive nor necessary, given adequate prior communication.

The plan must outline that data processing work which will be carried on at the offsite location in the event of the requirement to resort to the contingency plan. It must be anticipated that all the processing currently being carried on in the organization's computer room will not, in most cases, be accommodated at an offsite location. The organization's "critical" systems must be identified. These systems, once identified, must then be prioritized with the view to determining those which carry the greatest organizational impact. In the event of a disaster, a great deal of excitement and confusion is bound to occur; the decision as to what is, and what is not, to be processed must not be left to the computer operators.

Obviously, adequate remote site equipment must have been located and arrangements made to assure that that equipment be available, not only on short notice, but that it remain available for as long as may be required. The agreement which secures this remote site equipment must, of course, be in writing and must have been approved at levels in both organizations sufficiently high to assure compliance. While it is possible to effect "Mutual Assistance" agreements between organizations, it becomes increasingly apparent, given the increasing complexity of both equipment configurations and systems, that satisfactory arrangements of this nature will be difficult to maintain over time. As a practical matter, most organizations tend to maximize the use of their data processing equipment. This leaves little opportunity for any one else to obtain processing time of any significance.

Two rather recent developments provide options which offer more appropriate answers to the question of offsite backup facilities which are more appropriate than mutual assistance agreements. One of these options is the "shell" facility. This provides an opportunity to contract for space in a building which has been conditioned for the placement of data processing hardware. While the expense associated with the shell facility is low, the effectiveness of the concept is entirely dependent upon the delivery of replacement data processing equipment to the shell site by the equipment vendor. The key, of course, is to deliver that equipment as rapidly as possible! While all vendors will do their very best to deliver substitute equipment in the event of a disaster, and while their record of delivery has been very good, it can nonetheless require substantial time, even with the best of luck, to deliver, install, and bring the equipment to the proper operational level.

The second option, which while more expensive, yet provides greater security, is to enter into an agreement which provides access to a fully equipped, immediately available, remote site facility. This is much more effective, both in terms of being able to conduct the necessary periodic tests to determine that the plan, if required, can be effectively implemented (because these agreements provide for a given number of tests each year) and also provide the opportunity to resume operation quickly in the event of the occurrence of a disaster.

Consideration should be given to an option which may prove to be an effective solution in some organizations, that is the development of an in-company backup installation. This can be either a shell or a fully equipped site. The shell may consist simply of the identification of some remote company-owned location (remote may only be a block away) where sufficient space, power, air conditioning, and security can be provided to house data processing equipment on a temporary, yet immediate, basis.

The fully equipped, company-owned backup site is practical in those organizations which have several data centers. This can be accomplished in one of several ways. Redundant equipment could be installed in all data centers in the anticipation of a disaster in one location. Processing power in excess of that actually required, but less than completely redundant systems, could be installed at each location in order to carry a portion of the processing from a stricter data center. A third approach might be to build some flexibility into all data center schedules within the organization in order to take on some of the work of one of the data centers, should a disaster arise. In any event, none of these solutions are as effective or practical as a sound arrangement with a fully equipped commercial backup data center.

The ultimate choice depends, of course, on the perceived degree of risk associated with the contingency plan, and the willingness to allocate the required funds. Again, it is critical that senior management be aware of the alternatives, the expense, and the risk of each option. The higher expense associated with the fully conditioned and equipped backup site should not be cavalierly decided against. If disaster strikes, the expense associated with recovery, the ability to gain even a few days, perhaps a few weeks, in the recovery process will be worth the expense, not only in terms of dollars, but also in terms of the organization's image.

Given the increasing requirement to accommodate "data communications" processing, consideration of the computing "hardware" must not overlook the concomitant requirement to have appropriate telephone equipment available. Organizations which handle processing from remote locations, an increasingly important function in most installations, will find that their processing to and from those sites will be severely impaired without the availability of the required communications equipment at the remote site.

All agreements with outside locations, be they "mutual agreements," "shells," or fully developed "disaster centers," must be sanctioned by the organization's legal department. Data processors, as a group, have not demonstrated a particularly sound approach to dealing with legal considerations. Too much tends to be accepted on faith, on someone's word. This cannot be tolerated with a contingency agreement. When it is needed, the implementation of the agreement must be viable, enforceable, and swift. The organization's legal department, not the data processing department, must ensure that contingency contracts are valid, and that they remain valid.

An organizational "contingency plan team" must be set up. It may be appropriate to assign the overall responsibility for the team to someone outside the data processing department. Someone from the audit or security departments of the organization might be the appropriate people.

In addition to responsibility for the overall contingency plan, the team must also be charged with the responsibility for periodic tests of the plan. The results of these tests must be analyzed, and, where necessary, appropriate changes must be effected. The combination of changing data processing technology, new hardware or new software, in conjunction with the normal changes in the organization's method of conducting business will render portions of the contingency plan obsolete in a very short time.

The continual testing and updating of the plan can become bothersome; it may, in fact, become a greater effort than that of developing the original plan. It is, however, absolutely mandatory that the testing be carried on and that the required changes be made. Without this safeguard, the plan will become worthless in a very short time.

The rather general pattern of leaving the data processing problems and concerns of the organization (entirely) to the people involved in data processing is beginning, at last, to change! The belief that all aspects of data processing are too technical or too esoteric to be understood by members of senior management has never been valid. These beliefs are, particularly with regard to the subject of data processing contingency planning, spurious!

A growing awareness of the absolute requirement to install and maintain effective data processing contingency planning safeguards is developing. This awareness is not limited to the data processing departments; other sections of the organization are also beginning to realize the importance of adequate data processing contingency planning. An increasing number of backup site alternatives are being offered. A number of seminars dealing with the subject of contingency planning are offered each year. Not only is attendance growing, but it is not limited to those involved in data processing; members of auditing and security departments as well as members of senior management are attending in greater numbers.

It is simply a matter of time until some large organization suffers irreparable damage as the result of the loss of its data processing facility, and the concomitant inability to successfully recover. The real tragedy may not be the fact of the loss, but the fact that the loss was completely avoidable. A potential disaster can be transformed into an inconvenience through the implementation, testing, continual upgrading, and adequate documentation of a sound, strong contingency plan.

A new element has been introduced to this subject. The Foreign Corrupt Fair Practices Act of 1977* places increased responsibility on senior management for the safeguarding of information assets. The idea of the responsibility for the organization's data being the ultimate concern of the data processing manager is no longer adequate. Data processing contingency planning now becomes a higher level responsibility.

---

*The Corrupt Fair Practices Act of 1977 states in part that the management of an organization can face legal action if it can be proved that they have failed to adequately protect the organizations' data.

CHAPTER V
Feasibility

As the acceptance of automation in all aspects of office functions grows, as it becomes increasingly easier and less expensive to bring that automation to expanded areas of the organization, either as a part of the MIS function or as separate office automation functions, the pressure to either automate new processes or to improve the existing processes grows almost daily in many organizations. It is a fact that, as progress with the use of automation occurs, more and more uses will be found for automation. Because this is the case, and because computer resources even though becoming less expensive as they become more powerful are finite, what occurs is the development of sizable MIS project backlogs.

Today the average MIS recorded project backlog is in the area of three to five years. This does not include that "unadmitted" backlog of projects which are desired but which, because they know they have no chance of obtaining attention for them, people do not make a formal request for them, nor does it include any potential projects which might be undertaken outside the MIS department. Given the changing nature of most organizations, it is quite clear that, by the time some of the projects in the backlog are addressed, they may no longer be of value.

Because, as a practical matter, all projects cannot be developed and because of the subjectivity inherent in the issue of selecting projects which will be developed, some method must be instituted which will provide the facility to consider the individual merits of each proposed project. The goal here must be to enable those in management who must make the necessary decisions to make a reasoned determination about which projects should indeed be approved. There must be a method which will assist those involved in the selection process to determine the practicality and the real value of all proposed projects under consideration. The method used to make these determinations is the feasibility study.

Feasibility should not be confused with the process of proposing projects for preliminary consideration which should be done through the use of the Project Evaluation Sheet, described in another chapter. The question of feasibility should be considered after the preliminary decisions about projects have been considered and resolved by the MIS Steering Committee. The project evaluation process represents the "first cut" at identification of all possible projects. The feasibility process is the in-depth determination of the practicality, the cost, and the benefits of the projects which pass the first phase.

There are several considerations which must be kept in mind when the issue of feasibility arises. MIS project feasibility includes financial practicality (is the payback justified by the project; if not, are there overriding concerns; if so, what are they? and technical consideration (does the organization possess the technical skills, the hardware and software, and the people to make the project a success?). And there is the question of the "cultural" maturity of those who will use the system once it is in operation.

The question of the financial return on the money invested both in the development and ongoing operations of the system can be fairly easily determined through the standard cost/benefit analysis process. When this investigation is made, however, it is also important to consider nonfinancial considerations, such as the effect such a project may have on the organization's competition, as a factor in addition to a desired financial return as a basis for approval.

It may be that the financial return will be small, or perhaps even negative, yet the project may still be important enough to the organization that that approach makes good sense.

The issue of whether or not a proposed MIS project is truly feasible from a pure business standpoint is probably the most important consideration when attempting to determine the practicality of a particular project. However, this criteria is not always used in the selection of such projects. It is a fact that many organizations pay little, if any, attention to the process of determining the economic feasibility of projects. What often occurs is that many approved projects are the result of a forceful effort by strong managers to push their particular projects.

If the person pushing the project is high enough in the organization, there is little attempt on anyone's part to question the feasibility of the project; it is simply approved and implemented. Often the result is that the project fails, either economically, because it costs too much to develop and run, or technically, because it is beyond the current technical skills of the MIS department. In the first instance, because it was requested at a high level, the projects continue to be run. In the second instance, MIS will usually find itself paying a high price for such a situation. In many cases, because it cannot be done technically, after much time and expense the project will simply be abandoned.

MIS management can also be found to be a cause of the installation of projects which may not be in the best interest of the organization. It may be that a skillful MIS manager has been able to force a use of a new technology which does not have any relevance to the goals of the organization. It may be that the reason for such a move is simply because of the technical challenge of such a project. This is a situation which must be guarded against as carefully as any other when considering the feasibility of projects.

It is also correct that many times the desire to install new systems becomes an emotional issue, where the actual benefits to be obtained from the project become obscured in political arguments, either for or against the effort. While it is correct that there are often subtle benefits to projects, benefits which often are subjective, such as the adverse consequences with customers if a particular project is not approved and implemented, those benefits should be qualified through the feasibility process rather than accepted because of outside pressure.

While there is no way that anyone can be absolutely certain that an anticipated payback will be realized, there are methods which can be used to identify the costs and the payback to a reasonable extent. The idea is to develop a methodology which will assure that all proposed MIS projects are subjected to the same objective analysis and that the evaluation process is consistent.

Of course there will always be projects which, despite the result of the feasibility study, simply must be implemented. Some examples might include changes mandated by regulatory agencies which control the business environment in which the particular organizations operate. This is apparent in the banking and insurance industries where changes in regulations must be complied with; they are not optional. However, even in these instances, the feasibility study should be carried out because it helps point out possible alternatives and point up potential problem areas.

The project may indeed present a sound financial return for the required investment; but, does it impose technical constraints upon the organization which may be more than can be effectively handled by the MIS department? The questions raised should be: Are there appropriate technical skills available in the MIS department? Is there sufficient hardware available to carry on the work, particularly if the workload in the future increases? Is special software required to bring this project to fruition? What will be the total cost of these items?

The cultural concerns, both within the MIS department and perhaps more importantly the client departments, should not be ignored. There are any number of projects which should provide good payback, which do not present technical problems beyond the ability of the MIS department, but which never achieve the goals originally set for them.

The reason for these failures is often found in the unwillingness of those who must operate the system to accept their responsibility. Often these people continually fight the system, refuse to learn how to operate it correctly, and bring about its ultimate failure. This is not a reason to fail to implement projects; it is a matter to be addressed and corrected through management action. Being aware of the potential situation as a part of the feasibility study can assist in overcoming the problem before it gets out of hand.

An examination of these cultural problems may prove to be worthwhile. In many manufacturing operations there is both a strong desire and an acute need to install automated processes which will assist in the improvement of the particular organization's manufacturing process. One very effective method to address these problems is to install an MRP (Manufacturing Requirements Planning) system. While there are indeed great advantages to the implementation of such a system, and while the technical issues involved in the implementation, particularly if one of the currently available high quality software packages are used, are much less than might be expected, there are often very real problems involved in the installation of MRP.

One of these problems is the result of a failure on the part of those leading such a project to recognize the "cultural" problem which can make or break the project. If the paper flow in the current manufacturing process is not currently adequate, it must be improved prior to moving to a new computerized system. There may be a feeling, incorrect, yet often prevalent, that an MPR system can be installed quickly and for a very low price.

In order to be successful under such circumstances, time and energy must be devoted to the improvement of the current processes, be they manual or computerized, and to the development of a comprehensive plan which will assure that the basic groundwork has been carefully carried out prior to the installation of the computer software. A lengthy education process may be required within the manufacturing sections in order to obtain success.

In addition, members of the MIS department, particularly those who will have responsibility for the ongoing operation of the MRP system, must appreciate the need to operate the system carefully according to the instructions provided. If this is not done, a great deal of unnecessary expense and frustration will be encountered.

The MRP example represents a situation where several of the important components of feasibility are present; that is, the organization not only can, but is quite willing to spend the money on the system. The payback on this expenditure is very favorable. The technical skills and the hardware are available to successfully handle the project, yet it still will not be feasible because the organization is not culturally ready to accept this change.

While MRP, because of its almost universal potential for a positive payback, makes a good example of the cultural issue, it does not by any means represent a unique situation. The cultural aspect is a much more influential factor than is usually recognized in the success or failure of MIS projects. When MIS projects fail, it is usually MIS which is assessed the responsibility for the failure, that blame may be well deserved, yet it may also be that the cultural aspect of the project feasibility has been overlooked and that that is the real cause of the failure.

Unless care is exercised in the determination of the feasibility of projects what will happen, over time, will be the installation of a process which will foster a climate which encourages an environment of the "masterful manipulation of mushy data." This is, of course, a most undesirable yet not unusual circumstance. A great deal of MIS difficulty can be traced to a reluctance to carry out a thorough feasibility study prior to approval of an MIS project. Too often projects are approved and implemented without any attempt to justify their feasibility or determine their degree of probable success. The result, and there are far too many examples extant today, is an MIS system which not only does not serve its purpose, but which has cost so much, both in money and in emotional terms, that it continues to be used in spite of its faults.

The question of the technical feasibility of MIS projects is usually the easiest to address. The question, in its most elementary form, is simply whether or not the MIS department has sufficient hardware, software, and technical skills to competently handle the particular project. If those resources are not available, what will it cost to obtain them? These questions can be appropriately answered with relatively little effort in any well-managed MIS department.

The mechanics of preparing the material to address the requirements of the feasibility study for an MIS project are rather straightforward.

Examples of the types of documents used in the study are included as a part of this chapter. Some comments on the information to be included in those documents and processes involved may prove helpful.

It should be noted that the concept of a feasibility study should not be limited to MIS projects; it is valid for any type of project an organization might wish to consider. The concept is particularly important in dealing with the various issues of office automation which are now beginning to gain increasing momentum in most organizations.

The feasibility study should begin after a project has been approved by the organization's MIS Steering Committee and has been given a start date. The primary purpose of the feasibility study is to help determine the appropriateness of the particular project based upon the overall needs of the organization. The project evaluation sheet will have been used as a "first step" process to identify those projects which appear to carry a real value to the organization. As those evaluation proposals are reviewed by the MIS Steering Committee, a weeding-out process must be carried on so that only the most desirable projects are approved for future consideration.

These more desirable projects will, under the much more careful scrutiny of the feasibility process, come to be viewed as either worthwhile or unacceptable, based upon the other potential projects and the needs of the organization. The feasibility process is the detailed weeding-out effort to enable the organization's senior management to determine the desirability of that particular project.

There are two documents which should make up the feasibility study, they are, the Statement of Requirements and the Cost/Benefit Analysis. The primary responsibility for the preparation of these documents should lie, not with members of MIS, but with the nonMIS member of the project team who has been designated project leader. Members of MIS assigned to the project should, of course, participate in the preparation of the document and must furnish the technical information; but, the feasibility study must be basically the work of the nonMIS members of the team. This is in line with the assertion that MIS projects belong not to MIS but to the clients.

The purpose of the documents is to provide the members of the organization's Executive Committee the opportunity to evaluate the project on an objective basis. They should provide an improved understanding of the project to those who may not be familiar with its purpose. The documents must outline the scope of the project, its costs, both development and implementation, and ongoing operational costs, its benefits, both tangible and intangible, and the degree of risk inherent in the project.

The Statement of Requirements should outline the specific problem, or problems, which are to be addressed through the implementation of the project. This document will provide recommendations for solutions to those problems and should also consider practical alternatives.

The preparation of the Statement of Requirements has several purposes. One is to develop a vehicle which can be used to communicate to all interested or involved parties sufficient details about the ultimate goal of the project so that objective decisions can be made. A series of questions should be answered through the preparation of the Statement of Requirements. What is the problem or problems which will be addressed and corrected through implementation of the project? What new opportunities will be forthcoming as a result of the project? What specific steps are being recommended?

The Statement of Requirements must be as balanced a document as possible. That is, there must be sufficient detail to provide information about the proposed project to convey the purpose and result, yet not so much detail as to overwhelm those reviewing the report. It should be kept in mind that this is a document which is directed to a high management level within the organization and should be developed to accommodate that group.

An ancillary, yet perhaps an important, aspect of the development of the Statement of Requirements is that the process forces the members of the project team to think through the details of the project. This can prove to be a very valuable exercise. This is particularly true when those involved in the effort appreciate the need to carry out the exercise, keeping in mind the composition of the ultimate audience for the completed work.

The preparation of the Statement of Requirements can help impose an often much needed discipline into the process of developing MIS, or for that matter other projects within the organization. A very difficult, yet prevalent, problem in many MIS projects (and in all likelihood, any other type of project) is a tendency to focus on and then attempt to solve, not the problem itself, but symptoms of the problem.

As an example, an insurance company may find that their premium volume is declining. The apparent (perhaps the easy) answer to this problem may be to accede to the contention that policy rates are too high, that a lowering of the overall premium charge will solve the problem. As a result of such a superficial analysis, a project, perhaps a crash project may be instituted to reduce expenses in various sections of the organization so that rates, and in turn premiums, can be reduced in order to become more "competitive" and regain lost premium volume.

However, it may be determined on more careful analysis, through the effective use of a Statement of Requirements, that the cause of policy cancellations is not a result of policy costs, but due to a perception on the part of the company's insureds of a poor level of service. Given such a situation, a project to reduce expenses, while commendable, will not be at all effective here, because all that it will accomplish will be to lower the level of service which is already the cause of the difficulty.

This is a good example of the implementation of a project to solve a symptom, rather than a cause. In this case, and in many similar cases, this approach only exacerbates an already difficult situation. Carefully done, the Statement of Requirements can provide insights into these areas and can be extremely helpful in the identification of causes, rather than symptoms.

The second document, the Cost/Benefit Analysis, is prepared in order to demonstrate the practicality (or perhaps the lack of practicality) of the proposed project from the perspective of the "payback" or return on the funds being expended to develop and maintain the system. The project may indeed be feasible in all aspects, it may also be quite desirable; but, does it offer sufficient return on its investment to justify approval? Again, it may be, in spite of a failure to produce the desired rate of return, the project must, for any of a number of reasons, be approved. Even in these instances it is important to know the real cost of the project; the Cost/Benefit Analysis will produce that information.

Often, because of the usual euphoria generated by the introduction of a new project, particularly a project which has been long deserved, there is a tendency to ignore the Cost/Benefit Analysis process in order to move into the development stage of the project. The feeling may be, "the project must be worthwhile, we have waited so long for it we should not allow anything to delay the effort."

There is also a tendency to overlook or to minimize the ongoing costs associated with the project after it becomes operational. One argument which may be advanced is that this is not a particular consideration because the hardware and people are available anyway so the production expense is not an additional organizational cost. One factor must be kept in mind when such statements are made, sooner or later the cumulative effect of new projects will push the computing requirements past the point where any more processing increases can be accommodated.

At this point the equipment will have to be upgraded, or some of the existing work being processed will have to be removed from the system. This phenomenon of exceeding hardware capacity has a way of occurring very rapidly and without warning. The usual first indication of this situation is seen in a problem with CRT response time on the processing network. Correctly carried out, the Cost/Benefit Analysis can help avoid this problem.

One of the aspects of the Cost/Benefit Analysis is to identify the potential approach of an MIS capacity overload. With such information, the senior management group can be alerted to the fact that the cost of this particular project, if it requires increased hardware, may be more than had originally been anticipated.

A Cost/Benefit Analysis consideration with regard to a "make or buy" decision for the software portion of MIS projects is becoming increasingly important as an expanded array of high quality packaged software becomes available. The use of a high quality purchased software package, rather than attempt to design, code, program, test, and implement the software within the organization's MIS department, must be very carefully considered. Where good packages are available, they should be purchased and installed in preference to "in-house" development. In most cases, provided good software is purchased, the result will be a much more comprehensive, better documented, more reliable system which can be installed both more rapidly, and at less overall expense, than a "homegrown" version.

There are, however, several aspects of cost which cannot be ignored when considering the purchase of a software package. The initial purchase cost of the software is not the final expense. An annual maintenance fee, a percentage of the original purchase price, is assessed to provide the customer the opportunity to update the system with periodic enhancements.

In addition to the annual fee, the installation will have to provide a person who can apply the enhancements to the system and make certain they operate correctly. In the case of some packages, such as payroll, these enhancements, because both federal and state tax changes can be considerable, may become a full-time effort. Even with this additional expense, it is still better to buy a good package than to attempt to build one.

Of course, the enhancements to the purchased system can be ignored, just as enhancements to in-house developed systems can be ignored. The problem here is that, in most cases, failure to apply the required changes to a package within a specified time will invalidate the vendor support for the package. If, in such a situation, problems arise with the package itself, the vendor will usually not be willing to provide assistance until the requisite enhancements have been applied. In any event, a sound software package, correctly installed and maintained, is always preferable to building it in-house.

There is one concern with purchased software packages which must be kept in mind. In attempting to determine whether or not the package is of high quality, consideration must also be given to the aspect of the direction of the vendor with regard to applying the advances of technology to the product in the future. There are software packages available today which are of high quality, and which enjoy a very good and deserved reputation within the information processing industry; yet because these products are based upon technology which has become, or is becoming, obsolete, they may not be able to compete in the future. Care must be exercised in this area.

While the time spent on the investigation and preparation of the Statement of Requirements and the Cost/Benefit Analysis documents may be viewed in some quarters as a waste of time, or a prime example of MIS "red tape," they are necessary to the selection of MIS projects which will prove to be the most beneficial to the organization over time. The work involved can be tedious; it does require time and effort; yet if the organization is to effectively manage its information processing and obtain the best possible return on its information processing investment, it must be done.

CHAPTER VI
State of the Art

A great deal of time and attention is devoted within the MIS profession to the desirability of achieving and maintaining a state-of-the-art environment within the MIS department. While this is often, but by no means always, seen as a desirable goal, it has never been easy to accomplish. As the pace of technical change increases, the issue will become more prominent and will assume increasing importance in all organizations. It should be the resolve of every MIS manager, and of every member of the organization's senior management, to move as close as practical to the leading edge of the technology and once there, to make the required commitment in order to ensure that the organization maintains a state-of-the-art position.

It should be the stated goal of every MIS manager, regardless of the size of the organization, to adopt a concerted effort to make maximum use of the available technology in order to help drive the organization forward. The degree of success in a particular organization will often be something less than total, if for no other reason than because of the speed of technical change. However, the MIS manager must continue to press for the unrelenting movement toward that goal. The current benefits of such an effort (and the future benefits can be assumed to be much greater) mandate such a course of action.

While the benefits are so positive, the movement to a state-of-the-art environment should not be carried on in a cavalier manner, simply to make some type of "progress." To begin, the appropriate members of the organization must be made aware, not only of the real benefits to be derived, but also of the costs associated with movement to the state-of-the-art environment. These costs should not be measured in dollars alone;

the time and the frustration which will have to be endured to move ahead must also be acknowledged. Both the advantages and the disadvantages with moving to a state-of-the-art position must be understood by all involved, not just those in the MIS department, prior to embarking on such a process.

Conversely, the actual and the psychological costs associated with not moving ahead with the technology must also be realized. There is no such thing as maintaining the status quo in information management! Those MIS installations which are not progressing, not improving their service levels, are not standing still although that may appear to be the case; they are in fact falling behind. One reason why the uses of the new technology are not as prevalent as they should be in many organizations is simply due to either inertia or to fear on the part of the MIS management. It must be conceded that the effort to remain in a state-of-the-art position takes initiative; it requires a great deal of work; and there is always a degree of risk.

Of course, there is also the issue which must be faced by the MIS management which is that of attempting to convince an often skeptical senior management that the expense and organizational trauma of moving to and maintaining a state-of-the-art environment are indeed practical considerations for the organization. In those organizations where the issue has been ignored for a considerable time, the cost, trauma, and therefore the associated risk can indeed be high.

In this case, the degree of credibility which the MIS management group has been able to develop within the senior levels of the organization will help determine the ease with which the MIS management will be able to move to a state-of-the-art environment. Where credibility is high, even though the organization must make a considerable effort to move to a state-of-the-art position, if senior management has confidence in the MIS group's ability to do the work, the granting of permission to go ahead will be much more likely to occur.

Given the preceding, it can be seen that those organizations which fail to adopt a strong state-of-the-art orientation and then push consistently to reach and maintain that goal, make a serious mistake. That mistake will only come to be magnified as time moves on, there is just not any question but that those organizations which do not move to the state of the art will suffer long-term consequences.

There are several considerations with the issue of the state of the art. The usual concern is with the financial aspect. "We cannot afford the cost of advanced technology," is a rather common argument raised against the movement to the state of the art. This is, really, a spurious argument. It comes down, in the final analysis, to a "pay me now—or pay me later" situation. If the payment (the movement to a state-of-the-art position) is deferred, the final cost will always be greater; often far greater, than to have made the transition and remained at an advanced position early on.

The salient consideration is that sooner or later the money must be spent. When that spending begins, how large the expenditure is, and what is produced for the money, depends upon the particular organization, but delaying these expenditures will only increase the total cost. One point to keep in mind is that, the longer the delay the more there will be to convert to the advanced technology and therefore, the cost will also increase.

The question of what it will require to move to a state-of-the-art environment will, of course, carry different connotations in different organizations. These perceptions will to a great extent be reflections of the perception of the management of the MIS function. The usual interpretation of the state of the art is to refer to those areas where the most advanced, latest technological processes are being introduced and used. Currently, some examples might include robotics, computer-assisted design, satellite communications, data base management, and so forth. The interpretation often is used relative to whatever is considered at that time to be at the "leading edge" of the technology.

In actual practice, however, state of the art is a relative term. The approach to the development of a state-of-the-art stance must be modified to suit both the climate of the particular organization, and the status of the MIS technology within the organization at any given time. This includes the interest and the abilities of the people in the MIS department, and the willingness of senior management to actively support the effort. Some organizations have been at, and remain at, the leading edge; some organizations have been so remiss in this regard that they are really candidates for the term "stone age data processing."

It is often assumed that only the large organizations, because of their resources, can afford to stay at the leading edge of the technology. While it is correct that those organizations have more leverage in adopting such a position, every organization must determine what the context of the state of the art means to them and then must act accordingly. Every effort must be made to assess as accurately as possible the risks and the rewards associated with the state of the art, and the decision whether to move ahead or not must be based upon more than the financial considerations.

Unfortunately, the "leading edge" is often confused with the "bleeding edge." This often raises the specter of severe difficulties, of greatly increased potential for failure. While someone must be willing to accept what may

CHAPTER VI

prove to be extraordinary risk in order to break new ground, it is suggested that, if at all possible, someone else be allowed to take those really large risks. However, once the start-up problems have been solved and the technology is proven effective, those organizations which view the technology as practical should move to it.

An argument could be built for waiting, rather than move with every technological change, to avoid some of the problems encountered pushing to the edges of the technology. This may be a realistic approach in some instances. The difficulty can be found in the development of an approach which becomes a matter of waiting for the "next breakthrough," which may never come and the advantages to have been gained by moving earlier will be lost. Another problem is that often the waiting makes the process considerably more complex than to have carried it out in stages. There is no "best way"; each situation must be investigated and the most appropriate course selected. The salient consideration must be to remain aware of the need to continue to take the necessary action.

If an organization is to become a pioneer in some aspect of the technology (and of course if the process is to become practical someone must take the risk), there should be a compelling reason to do so. If the decision is made to go ahead to develop new technology, the vendor involved in the effort, and who will stand to gain if the process is successful, should be willing to accept a large portion of the risk inherent in the process. Any assurances from the vendors that risk will be minimal in these new, untried technologies, should be treated with appropriate skepticism.

Many MIS managements have not yet learned that the smooth assurances of the vendor's salespeople may not become reality in the hands of the vendor's technicians. As is the case with any substantial change, the issues must be very carefully assessed. The ultimate decision to go ahead or not must be arrived at after the appropriate information has been developed and analyzed. Reliance upon the representatives of the vendor's sales force has not always proved to be the best course for the organization to take.

While it is often the larger organizations which have moved to the uses of advanced technology, which have been willing to assume leading edge (if not bleeding edge) positions, that does not mean that simply because an organization is large that it has developed a state-of-the-art position. Many, far too many, large organizations do not devote sufficient time and attention to the development of a true state-of-the-art environment.

The preferred approach, with regard to the use of advanced technology in many organizations, size being irreverent, is to simply maintain the status quo. When the managers of these installations are asked why they have not made any effort to move their MIS functions ahead, it is usual to hear responses about the new technology being "too expensive," "not a good fit for our organization," or "too unstable." While these may be valid reasons, it is also correct to surmise that fear or perhaps simple inertia, or both, play a rather important part in the failure to use the new technology.

This, of course, is a reflection of the mind set of a particular type of MIS management. The adoption of such a stance does not mean that new technical opportunities will be investigated and evaluated and those which prove effective will be used; it means that nothing new is going to be attempted. This is a decidedly unfortunate situation for the organization. However, there should be hope. What often occurs is that, sooner or later, the MIS problems will swell to a point where new management will take over and, hopefully, progress toward a more productive environment will begin.

The turnover among MIS managers has and continues to be high. There are a number of reasons for this; but a significant cause of dissatisfaction by senior management, although they may not be completely aware of the cause, is the inability of MIS to provide the required services to its clients. Much of the cause of this problem is based upon the MIS department's unwillingness to adopt more effective state-of-the-art processes.

The place to begin, when considering the particular strengths or weaknesses of any organization in terms of the effective use of the technology, is from the perspective of that which is actually being done currently within the MIS department; and perhaps more importantly, the attitude of the MIS department manager concerning the issue. An important question must be, "What is the relation of the particular organization to the industry in general, with regard to the available technology?"

The question has several facets. What is available? How can use of the advanced technology serve the organization? What is the current status of the MIS department in terms of overall technical approach? How far behind the accepted state of the art is the organization, three years, five years? Five years may appear to be a long time; and indeed it is, yet there are organizations which, by any measurement, would have to be considered to be eight to ten years behind the current state of the art.

There is some criteria which can be helpful in the determination of the position of the particular organization relative to the state of the art. The application of these items to a particular installation can help provide information with which to make an informed assessment about the magnitude of the effort to move ahead.

Some of those items are:

- Heavy use of "batch" processing and punched cards.
- Little, perhaps no, availability of on-line programming facilities.
- Restricted ability for the testing of new and changed programs. That is, the introduction of improperly tested systems or new programs into the production environment.
- Too much concern with the efficient use of "hardware resources," to the detriment of the organization.
- Reliance upon early generation hardware.
- Obsolete operating software.
- Lack of effective project reporting and control functions.
- A process which supports the in-house development of large projects, as opposed to the purchase of commercial applications software packages.
- A lack of cross training.
- Poor, perhaps no, documentation, and little effort to correct that situation.
- No support for the continued technical training of members of MIS.
- Limited, or ineffective, long-range MIS planning.
- Failure to attempt to position the MIS effort with the goals of the organization.

This is by no means a complete list, but it is intended to provide some idea of the type of items which need to be considered in the attempt to determine an organization's state-of-the-art commitment. Of course, any analysis of this type must be as objective as possible. In many organizations, particularly those which have demonstrated a decidedly backward approach, the use of outside consultants will prove to be most beneficial in the identification of issues and to suggest new, improved methods which can help move the organization to a state-of-the-art environment.

The goal of this process should be to move the organization ahead. It should not become a witch hunt to fix blame. While some analysis of the causes of the failure to move ahead may be helpful, that should not be the primary concern. The purpose must be to assess the current MIS function, relative to the state of the art, and then lay out a plan for improvement. Often it is assumed that the complete responsibility for failure to move to the state of the art rests with the management of the MIS function. This may indeed be the cause; however, it may not be the total reason, and action against the MIS manager should be delayed until all the facts are known. It may well be that responsibility for the failure rests with the organization's senior management's failure to provide adequate support for the endeavor.

In those installations where the MIS function can be classified as "stone age," the cost to move to a state-of-the-art environment, and the time required to accomplish that goal can be massive. Presenting such information to a senior management group cannot be described as a pleasant task, yet it is something which must be done. A point which is often overlooked in such discussions, yet one which is quite valid, is that the organization has spent a great deal of time, and probably a great deal of money, to arrive at the current deplorable state. It is only logical then, having to undo the situation will require time, money, and perhaps most importantly, patience, if the situation is to be turned around.

The term state of the art is really a relative term. Moving closer to a more advanced environment means different things to different installations. As an example, an organization which makes heavy use of punched card processing and of second generation computing hardware, may see movement to greatly reduced use of punched cards and the installation of current level hardware as a dramatic step forward in terms of the state of the art. In this particular organization that effort may represent a valid position, while in a more sophisticated installation something much more complex may represent a state-of-the-art position.

The effort to move to a state-of-the-art position in an organization where little has been done to remain near the leading edge for years will of course be traumatic. The cost will be high, but part of that price will be that which must be paid as an offset to the money which has been "saved" over the years by not having moved to a more sophisticated stance in the past.

Many times there is a subtle reason for the failure to move to a more advanced technical position within an organization. Because the impetus for such a change would normally begin within the MIS department, in addition to the normal resistance to change, the maintenance of the status quo is often seen as a method by which members of MIS can increase their job security.

In those installations where the data processing is carried on through the use of obsolete techniques, where documentation is nonexistent, where all the information about systems and often about how they are run, is carried around in the heads of the members of MIS, who in all likelihood have considerable tenure, there is little incentive to change. In these situations, the installation management often fails to provide any type of cross training, which allows employees to develop a "lock" on certain processing aspects, and there is no one else who can make the system work if it fails, or change it when required.

Given such a situation, those employees have a distinct advantage. Since the MIS function would in all likelihood unravel without these people and since they see no compelling reason to adopt new technologies, the movement to a state-of-the-art environment must come from outside the MIS department. Under these circumstances the situation will only become increasingly worse as time moves on, it is now the responsibility of senior management to take whatever action may be required to correct the problem and begin the process to build a more sophisticated MIS function.

Another aspect of this "stone age" processing approach is that the applications system portfolio will probably be very old. Absolutely critical systems will be found to be ten, twelve, or perhaps even more, years old. The programming languages these systems are written in may now be obsolete (with only a very limited number of people, perhaps only one in the department having an understanding of the language.) It may be that these languages will not process on newer equipment, so that, even if the organization does want to move to new, more sophisticated hardware, it cannot be done without a rewrite of these systems.

Given the preceding litany of problems, and what might be viewed as excessive expense associated with the effort to move to and remain at a state-of-the-art environment, why would anyone want to do so? Some of the more compelling reasons are:

- The rate of change in the technology, both the hardware and the software, is very rapid and that rate of change is accelerating. Not remaining somewhere near the leading edge of the technology causes serious problems and additional expense.
- Not only technical changes, but also competitive forces can impact the value of the organization's application software portfolio. As software becomes increasingly flexible, astute organizations which have taken advantage of these new techniques will be able to provide increased customer service, which will provide a significant competitive edge.
- The effective use of advanced technologies can produce dramatic reductions in many expense areas within an organization. With careful thought and planning, the money spent on the advanced technologies can produce positive, often dramatic, returns on those investments.
- As the technology (both hardware and software) changes, the support provided by the vendors becomes less. While the preferred stance with regard to the installation's software, both operating and application, is to be as independent of the vendor as possible, being too far behind the technology places too much dependency on particular employees within the MIS department, if they leave and the vendor no longer supports critical software packages, chaos will occur. What usually happens as a result, is that the organization enters into a "crash" campaign to the new technology, often at more expense than if a rational, phased approach were used.
- The ability of the MIS department to provide increasingly sophisticated solutions to organizational problems, solutions which can help move the organization ahead in many areas will simply not be available. Many of these technolo-

gies are complex and require lead time to be effectively used; there can be severe competitive disadvantages to delay.
- The ability of the organization to attract and retain the high quality person required to support its objective can be severely constrained if these people do not view the particular organization as being at, or near the state of the art. While this is apparent in the MIS department, it is becoming more of a problem in other areas of organization. Those organizations which employ engineers are finding, without adequate computer technology, high grade prospects are not interested in employment.

There are always a number of issues which are raised in an attempt to forestall the introduction of new technologies. One which is often mentioned is the long lead time required to install sophisticated technology, particularly in "stone age" installations. Often some stopgap measure is employed which, while it reduces the time required to make some progress, usually proves to be less than satisfactory over time. This is usually not a true movement to a state-of-the-art environment, but merely a somewhat updated version of the old Jerrybuilt processes. It does take a long time to install some aspects of the state-of-the-art technology; however, the longer the organization delays, the longer it will take to realize any real benefits.

There is often a psychological aspect to the introduction of improved information management techniques in organizations where little has been done to move ahead. In those organizations a type of atrophy sets in, resistance to change, to new ideas, becomes an overriding condition. The NIH (not invented here) syndrome sets in, unless that is the way it has always been done, or unless "we" thought it up, it cannot be any good. New ideas or concepts are not applicable in the organization; they "won't work here" becomes an often heard theme.

Such a condition is both self-perpetuating and self-defeating. In time, a growing resistance not only to change, but, more importantly, to the acceptance of risk, develops. People begin to feel that the "safe" way is the best way. When these conditions are in force, the ability to move to the new technologies to make progress will be stifled. Management, both MIS management and the organization's senior management, must work to encourage a reasonable degree of risk taking, to be patient, and to accept an occasional delay or disappointment as part of the price of progress.

In those organizations where little has been done to remain current with the technology, sooner or later, some issue will cause senior management to take an interest in the subject of movement to a state-of-the-art position. What may cause such a situation? Any number of occurrences, or a combination of several desperate occurrences, usually begin the process. Some examples may be worth considering.

Senior executives may discover that their competition is working in advanced areas, such as teleworking, satellite communications, electronic mail, robotics, or word processing, and that these functions are providing real competitive advantages. They may be subjected to "hard sells" from vendors. Or, the frustration level with operational problems may grow to the extent where "something better" must be put in place.

At this juncture, it is often the case that cost and effort may be overlooked in the desire to "clean up the MIS mess," or to "gain control over MIS." It may also be that the question asked will be "what are we getting for the money we are spending on our MIS effort?" Often the answer is "not much." The "pay me now—pay me later" syndrome is now in effect.

The fear that the MIS function is "out of control" has several different connotations. It may revolve around the fact that too little actual control of the operational aspect of the information management process is in place. This is usually brought to the fore by work done by the various audit groups which review the MIS function, or by the continued failure of the MIS department to deliver the work assigned in a consistent manner.

"Out of control" may also be used to imply that the thrust of the MIS department effort is not viewed as being in line with the goals of the organization. This is usually apparent in the inability of the MIS function to accommodate the changing requirements of the organization. Often this phenomenon appears in the area of the organization's marketing or customer service functions, where change is often, and it is sometimes dramatic.

Both of these "out of control" situations are usually reflections of a less than state-of-the-art MIS effort. Both can be improved through the development of sophisticated techniques. The appropriate application of various technologies will greatly enhance both the control of the day-to-day operational aspects of the MIS function, and the ability of MIS to respond. It may require new MIS management, with new ideas, and an aggressive attitude to make the desired progress.

Once into a mode which adopts a stance of "We never did it that way before," it will often require a change of MIS management which will be required to take a very firm position in order to break the MIS department out of its lethargy. It may indeed require notice to some long-term employees that it is in the best interest of everyone concerned if they find other employment. The movement to the state of the art will be difficult enough in such an environment, without being forced to deal with excessive resistance from the entrenched, "old-timers."

The feeling that movement to a state-of-the-art environment is too expensive, is really a relative term. The basic question which must be posed with regard to expense as it pertains to the state of the art is, "What does the organization want, when does it want it, are those expectations realistic, and then, what will that cost?" This issue must be given careful consideration; it may well be that delay in these efforts will prove, in the long run, much more expensive than would a strong commitment to the technology.

The cost of moving to the state of the art can, of course, be high. As has already been stated, the cost is dependent upon what has, or has not, been accomplished in the past. However there is an almost standard rule of information management, that is, that change will not only continue, it will become more rapid. Movement to the state of the art is not a one time situation; it is a constant, unremitting effort. Any organization unwilling to face that fact and to make appropriate accommodations will face great difficulty.

While the preceding may be viewed as an unpleasant situation in many organizations, it is a fact of information management life. Failure to accept that fact and to produce plans and strategies which will, over time, address the issue of the appropriate use of technology, and to direct its use to the good of the organization is very shortsighted. Such a position is really futile.

If for no other reason, one clear fact indicates that this constant change and improvement of the new technologies will only grow more rapid. That fact is the competition among the vendors of the technology, both hardware and software. Vendors, pushed by their competitors, must continue to offer more, at less expense, which will also mean a growing expense to maintain obsolete technology, which of course means its demise. When this happens, the vendor will simply, from an economic consideration, drop the old technology. The vendors are, to a great degree, as much the victims of the new technology as the customers. They, too, are continually forced to move ahead.

MIS management has a clear responsibility to point out to senior management the fact that the state-of-the-art question is a "moving horizon." Because the technology changes so rapidly, because the need to remain current can, and in the future certainly will, become so acute, the expense associated with the effort will be ongoing. The ideal way, the most cost-effective method in the long run, may be to move to the state of the art and stay there.

Using a phased approach which recognizes the requirement to carry on a continuous effort to remain near the state of the art will not only prove to be less expensive in the long run than "saving money" for years and being faced with gaining ground in a hurry, but the benefits of using advanced technology will be available on a continuing basis. This approach will build expertise which can then be used to gain even more benefit from the technology than will be the case in the instances of "crash" projects.

Small installations develop a tendency to become complacent about the need to move to a state-of-the-art environment. They will often protest that they have neither the resources nor the need to adopt a state of the art position. They may maintain, because they have few changes to their systems, that little need arises to move to more sophisticated processes. That is not correct! The requirement to become and to remain aware of new developments in the technology are universal; the size of the organization is immaterial. While the scale and the magnitude are of course different, depending upon the size of the installation, the need is no less immediate in the small installation than in the large installation.

Small MIS installations are microcosms of large MIS installations. The forces at work with regard to automation affect small installations just as severely as they do large installations. There is also the factor of growth. With few exceptions, all MIS installations tend to become larger and increasingly complex over time, often over an amazingly short time. In addition, the question of obsolescence, because of the smaller staff, may be a more critical issue in the small installation. Large organizations may be able to handle obsolescence because they have, or are able to obtain, the skills and tools required to overcome the problems of obsolescence. The small organization, dependent upon a vendor to support obsolete hardware or software, is in for a very rude shock when the vendor announces withdrawal of support for those products.

The issue of software is being recognized as an increasingly important aspect of the development of a state-of-the-art environment. There are two separate considerations in the general area of software: operating software, that is that software which controls the functions of the equipment, and the operation of the applications software, which is that body of programs which produce the information required by clients of the MIS function. The subject of operating software is somewhat more technical than is desirable for this discussion, suffice it to say that this software will, in all probability, become increasingly complex. Conversely, it will also become increasingly flexible and will provide improved equipment and application productivity. The considerations with operating software are the same as those of any other state-of-the-art concern; the recommendation is to move to as close to the leading edge as practical, and then make a strong commitment to remain at the leading edge.

Application software is a subject which needs some elaboration. Many organizations are now facing a "make or buy" situation in almost every new MIS development project being considered. The resolution of the question often poses a dilemma. Often, members of the MIS department will resist the introduction of any process which moves away from the complete development of systems within the organization. The rationale is apparent, although not always expressed. The design, development, and implementation of large, complex MIS projects is viewed within MIS as the most exciting, challenging, and rewarding aspect of MIS work. This is seen as an opportunity to be creative, to develop new skills, and, importantly, to build the resume.

Often the MIS clients will also raise protests when the introduction of new projects are recommended to be carried out with the use of purchased software packages, rather than developed in-house. One of the most often voiced positions of those in the client departments is that while the use of a particular package may be fine for other organizations, "We are too unique to be able to use such an approach here." This is usually a spurious argument and is reflective of an unwillingness to change methods, to accept new solutions to problems.

Any organization which does not give strong and serious consideration to the procurement of good applications software packages whenever possible is not accepting the best available method of making MIS progress. Time, money, and frustration, often a great deal of frustration, can be saved through the selection and implementation of sound application packages.

There are several caveats which need to be kept in mind in dealing with the question of the use of purchased application software. While there are a number of very good packages, there are also some which are not of high quality; care must be exercised in the selection process. In addition to the obvious technical and functional considerations, the vendor's financial strength should be investigated. This financial investigation should not be done within MIS, but by someone else in the organization with financial skills.

Members of MIS and the client departments which will use the system must consider and obtain satisfactory answers to questions such as the degree of state-of-the-art techniques used in the system; some packages are very good, but they use obsolete techniques. As an example, does the vendor interface with currently used data base management systems? If not, are there plans to do so, when? What is the level of ongoing system support once the application package is installed? Conversations with other customers of the vendor and the use of one of the several commercial rating services will help provide the required information.

Again, the caution against reliance upon the salespeople when considering the selection of a new software package must be raised. Assurances that new, desirable, techniques are soon to be made available must be treated with a degree of skepticism. While the salesperson may be absolutely sincere about these representations, results rest with people in the technical section of the organization, over whom the sales department probably has little control. It is much better to see the process in operation than to be comfortable with assurances from the sales department.

Because applications software packages are designed to cover a variety of general situations, it will often be maintained, even if there is agreement to purchase a particular package, that modifications should be made to accommodate the organization's peculiar needs. This should be resisted as strongly as possible. In those organizations where agreement has been reached to install the package "as is" for ninety days and then consider modifications, it usually occurs that once the clients become familiar with the system they forget about modifications. The reason is that the application package, provided it is a good one, will do a much better job than the former system.

While the savings in development time and effort can be considerable with a purchased application software package, there is a cost which is not entirely apparent, but which must be recognized. Periodically the vendor will send enhancements to the system. These enhancements may range from something quite minor, which can be done in a very short time, to massive changes or complete new versions of the system. The massive changes can easily consume several man-months of effort to install, test, and implement. This effort is not restricted to the MIS department; the clients will also have to be involved.

If these changes are not installed in a timely fashion, the vendor may not provide ongoing support for the system, even though the annual maintenance fee has been paid by the customer. Organizations need to recognize this cost prior to the installation of the package. With an internally developed system, enhancements can be held to an absolute minimum, if so desired. The resources devoted to the required support of applications packages can become considerable if a number of packages are installed. Even with the above cost, the installation of good application software packages can be more cost effective than in-house development, and will help the organization move to and remain in a state-of-the-art environment.

One aspect of a state-of-the-art environment which is often overlooked, yet which is important is the absolute requirement to make and to maintain a strong commitment to MIS documentation. This is a subject which has been given much attention, and much lip service, during the past several years. It is probably safe to speculate that most organizations MIS documentation efforts range from poor to nonexistent. It would be impossible to calculate the additional cost imposed upon organizations as a result of poor documentation.

The causes of this lack of effective management of MIS documentation are varied, but the primary cause has been a lack of resolve on the part of MIS management to establish and enforce strong documentation standards. The high and rapid rate of MIS employee turnover, coupled with the rapid rate of technical change, mandates sound MIS documentation. There are a number of at least semiautomatic functions to help improve MIS documentation; they should be used.

Because documentation is a valid part of the MIS effort, wherever possible, the computer should be used to assure that the required documentation is in place. The use of the data dictionary function can provide great benefits in this endeavor. There is a real problem within most MIS departments, which is that the computer is not appropriately used to solve MIS problems. What might be described as the "shoemaker's children" syndrome is in effect in many MIS departments.

One reason for the high rate of personnel turnover in MIS departments, and there are a number of reasons, is the interest of the employees in learning to use the advanced technologies. This is a quite understandable interest. No one wants to be faced with a set of skills which have little practicality, or marketability. While the development of a state-of-the-art environment will not guarantee reduced turnover, it will help, and it will also be an important factor in the organization's ability to attract and retain high quality MIS people; a factor which will become increasingly important in the future.

There is an important corollary between the state-of-the-art issue and the attraction and retention of high caliber MIS employees. If a state of the art cannot be built and maintained without good people, good people cannot be encouraged to join "stone age" installations.

Movement to, and a commitment to remain near, the leading edge of the state of the art carries with it a degree of risk, additional expense, and will certainly engender some chaos. The expense is something which simply must be recognized and borne. The risk and the chaos can, through the use of sound planning and control be, not eliminated, but effectively reduced. The key is the development and use of a long-range plan which not only recognizes the requirement to adopt a supportive attitude toward a more sophisticated approach, but to also aggressively pursue such an approach. This must be a comprehensive plan, which has as its goal the practical application of state-of-the-art techniques.

There is an alternative to the work of developing an effective long-range state-of-the-art plan; one which, unfortunately, is adopted by too many organizations. This approach is to simply do nothing. Sooner or later the result of this approach pays its dividends and then begin the recriminations and effort to "clean up the mess." Better to face up to the issue and move to correct the problems before they become worse.

Facing the issues involved in using advanced technologies will take determination. The MIS management must be willing to provide the required leadership. A number of objections can be anticipated; they must be dealt with as they arise. In order to be successful, the support of the organization's senior management must be secured. Because this may be a totally unexpected issue, members of senior management may, if the costs are high and the length of time required high, react with shock and dismay.

The most effective approach is for MIS management to address the issue head on. The development plan must detail, not only the costs, the time, and the risks involved, but also the anticipated benefits which will be obtained. Those benefits, insofar as possible, must be associated with the goals of the organization, not as esoteric technical advances. The plan, while recommending a specific approach, should also address possible alternatives and explain the strengths and weaknesses of each.

The plan must be carefully thought through. It must be so structured that, insofar as can be anticipated, all the bad news is brought out as early on as possible. As the planning progresses, as the magnitude of the effort becomes better understood (and perhaps begins to overwhelm the planners), the tendency will be to attempt to mitigate the situation by deferring a portion of the bad news for a later period. This is a mistake! Credibility is one of the most important attributes an MIS department can develop; every effort, no matter how painful, must be pursued to develop and maintain a high degree of MIS credibility. The MIS manager has an absolute responsibility to "tell it like it is"; this is a responsibility which must not be taken lightly.

As a practical matter, the issue of moving to a state-of-the-art environment, once it is raised, will bring forth the fact that there is a plethora of options. This may come to be as much a negative as a positive factor. Often an attempt begins to investigate all the options available, to make "certain" that the very best approach will be found. What then occurs is a delay in the actual movement to the state of the art. This happens due to what becomes the excessive effort to "analyze" all the options. In order to make progress, the process should be to investigate as carefully as possible that which is available, choose what appears to be the best, and go with that choice.

Many MIS managers spend too much time in worrying about being second guessed. They have to move away from looking over their shoulders and become more decisive. The fact is that, later on, someone will in all likelihood question, if not attack, decisions which have been made, hindsight is always 20/20; the MIS manager must accept some mistakes as part of the territory. On balance, everyone will be further ahead when the MIS manager adopts and continues to strive for, a state-of-the-art environment.

CHAPTER VII
The Information Center

The term the Information Center has gained a great deal of attention within Management Information Services (MIS) departments during the past several years. While the specific meaning of the term is subject to interpretation within any given organization, the basic concept is to more effectively utilize large-scale data processing equipment so as to provide increased direct data processing capacity to the clients of the MIS department.

The Information Center is, in reality, an in-house time sharing, or interactive processing facility. The context in which the term will be used for the purpose of this discussion is as follows, "The Information Center is designed to better utilize the power of large-scale data processing hardware and state-of-the-art technology (both hardware and software); and the technical capabilities of people within the MIS department to serve all departments of the organization."

The Information Center effort must be viewed as a coalition between MIS and its clients to move toward a much more effective, more responsive, data processing environment. The goal should be to create an environment where the MIS clients enjoy an increased opportunity to better control and manage a certain spectrum of their information processing requirements on their terms and at their own pace.

The impetus toward the Information Center concept is the result of several factors. Advances in technology, both in hardware, in terms of reduced cost, and in software, in terms of an expanding array of "user friendly" programming languages, have made the concept much more practical than had been the case even several years ago. These circumstances will continue to operate to make the Information Center an increasingly attractive option in the future.

The increasing availability of small computers (micro processors), which are easy to use, relatively inexpensive, and very powerful, have forced many MIS managers to give serious thought to the type of service they offer, and to consider alternatives which will prove to be more beneficial to those outside the MIS department. The introduction of these small processors, which are under the complete control of those outside the MIS function, have often been viewed by these people as the only viable alternative to solving many of their data processing problems.

In many organizations the growth of these small processors has come about as a reaction to the dissatisfaction with the level of service provided by the MIS department. The typical problems encountered with MIS, at least from the client's point of view, center on issues such as long lead times to develop new systems, inflexibility on the part of the MIS department, too much MIS complexity, and a perception that MIS has not demonstrated an interest in adapting business solutions to the problems posed by the clients. In addition, many clients hold the view, often justified, that their organization's MIS department is simply unresponsive to their immediate needs.

It is certainly no secret that in many organizations there exists a decided lack of confidence and trust of MIS on the part of those who use the services provided by MIS. Often this is justified, many MIS departments are too concerned with the technology and do not adopt sufficient interest in the marketing of MIS.

However, MIS is not entirely to blame. Part of the perception of an unresponsiveness on the part of MIS, is due to the requirement of the centralized MIS function to impose necessary controls and constraints in order to provide a consistent level of service. While these controls and constraints are necessary, and in some installations are too lax as it is, the enmity of the clients is heightened by the failure of the MIS department to adopt a sales orientation toward the client base. All too often, MIS takes an imperious stance, which does its image great harm.

Unfortunately, there are numerous instances in the typical organization of MIS clients being subjected to displays of arrogance on the part of members of the MIS department. While many times this is done without malice, the message which comes across to the MIS client is clear, "We are not really interested in helping you."

The failure of MIS to establish a base of mutual trust and understanding with its clients, and often with the organization's senior management as well, has had a deleterious effect upon its perceived performance. This has been further exacerbated by the fostering within most MIS departments of the idea of the "mystic" of the MIS function. The attitude often expressed by members of MIS, in not so subtle forms, that the work being carried on in MIS is so complex, so esoteric, that only the anointed have the power to comprehend that which is being carried on in MIS, only helps to widen the gulf between MIS and its clients.

When these rather common facts are considered, it is understandable that the MIS clients, frustrated in their attempts to procure what they feel are acceptable results from MIS, are willing to install small computers (with, of course, the willing assistance of the vendors) and to attempt to do the work they feel must be done on their own.

Several factors, aside from the declining expense of the personal computer, have made the use of this equipment an increasingly attractive alternative for these client departments. The vendors of this equipment have gone to great lengths to convince those outside the MIS department of the advantage of the equipment. A great deal of thought and effort have gone into making the use of this equipment as straightforward as possible.

This increased "user friendly" aspect of personal computers has obviously done much to enhance their appeal to people with little or no prior data processing experience. While more work remains to be done in this area, improvements are being made every day. Many vendors have adopted an approach which demonstrates an interest in the problems faced by potential customers, and have worked to cultivate their trust. This has also helped promote the use of personal computers.

Another phenomenon is occurring which is accelerating the demand for increased direct data processing, whether through the use of personal computers or the Information Center. An increasing percentage of people entering the work force, regardless of their educational background, are not only familiar and comfortable with computers, but they expect to have direct computer power available to them as a part of their normal business environment.

This trend will certainly accelerate as the use of direct data processing power becomes common at all levels of business. This is something which should not be overlooked by organizations. In the future, those organizations which do not or will not provide direct computing power as a more or less routine office tool, will find it increasingly difficult to attract and hold high caliber people, not only in the MIS departments, but in other departments as well.

As a consequence, senior management in many organizations face, or will face, a dilemma. The problem, stated in rather basic terms, is to accede to the growing demand within the organization for increased data processing power at the client level, to use that power in such a fashion as to increase productivity and employee satisfaction, yet at the same time, to maintain reasonable control of the process and, most importantly, maintain both the control and integrity of the organization's data.

This dilemma presents serious problems for all levels of an organization's management. While the magnitude of this problem is not yet apparent in many organizations, it is real and must be faced. The reason little attention is being paid to the problem is because most organizations have not yet moved far enough along with either personal computers or the Information Center so that the issues have surfaced. However, it is certain to be an issue, often a serious issue, in all organizations in the future.

The answer to the problem can be stated in simple terms, "provide data processing power directly to the client, yet ensure avoidance of the creation of an 'out of control' situation." While the answer may be simple, the management of the problem is not.

Often the movement to the use of personal computers has been carried out in a circumspect manner. Because the entry level expense for this equipment is small, many department managers are able to obtain the equipment on their own authority. In other situations, particularly in departments with a strong engineering thrust, component parts have been purchased under some guise, such as miscellaneous calculator parts, and have then been assembled into personal computers.

The results of these efforts, in terms of the client being able to assume more direct control of his data processing needs, and in many instances increased productivity, cannot be denied. In many instances the results produced from these endeavors have been dramatic. In some organizations the results have been so positive that the clients have made their efforts public knowledge and have obtained official management support.

Clearly, however, the issue of control, both of the data processing hardware and of the organization's data, has been circumvented. There have been occasions where the senior management of an organization has been shocked to find that there are a number of computers within the organization of which they were not, nor was the manager of MIS, aware. When this occurs, most senior management groups will feel that they do indeed face an "out of control" situation. Often at this juncture, the tendency is to overreact which may, in the long run, do more harm than good.

The onus for much of this condition must rest with the management of the organization's MIS department. Many client department managers have felt they have had no choice other than to attempt to accommodate their immediate data processing needs in whatever manner would produce results. Often they have felt their only option was to install their own equipment.

This has come about because the position of MIS has often been that they cannot, or will not, provide the required support for more direct use of large scale data processing power by their clients. In addition, they have done everything possible to forestall the movement to any alternative methods which might offer solutions to those clients. Faced with this intransigence, managers of the client departments have reacted as one might expect; they have devised their own solutions. Where necessary, this has occurred outside of the organization's rules.

This circumstance poses serious concern for the organization. The issues here revolve around the question of control. Not only control of expenditures as they pertain to the acquisition of small computers, or of the control and availability of the organization's data, but also of the control and coordination of the work being carried on within the organization. While this may be nothing more than a minor irritant in some instances, there is always the potential for it to become a serious problem. There is no question, unless adequate control is imposed and proper support provided, these issues will become major concerns in many organizations. The time when this will occur is fast approaching in many organizations. The time to face them is now!

The preceding has been used to develop an explanation of the situation an increasing number of organizations are certain to find themselves in in the near future. The intent of this chapter is not to make judgment about the desirability or effectiveness of small computers located in, and totally under the control of, departments outside MIS. There is no right or wrong answer to that issue; it must be faced and resolved in each organization, based upon the facts as they apply within that organization.

The salient issue must be that the appropriate level of the organization's management must be aware of what is being done, of both the potential benefits and consequences of these actions and their ramifications, not only in the particular client department, but throughout the organization. Senior management must also be aware of the inherent dangers involved in allowing the uncontrolled growth of these activities.

Any organization which is not willing to face these issues and to take the steps required to resolve them is simply being remiss. These issues will not go away; they will not become less important. While they may not be readily understood by many members of senior management, they must not be ignored.

As a first step, all organizations, regardless of size, must develop and support a policy which outlines the appropriate uses of data processing equipment within the organization. The policy must outline specific duties and responsibilities and it must address the issue of the provision of direct data processing functions. Again, the specifics of the policy statement must be determined by the characteristics of the particular organization.

Some questions need to be asked. Is a policy against the use of personal computers appropriate for this organization? Should everyone be allowed to do as they please with regard to data processing? Is some combination of these two extremes the answer? It depends, of course, on the direction provided by senior management; the primary objective must be to formulate and install a policy which will provide direction and the appropriate (for that organization) level of control.

The details and direction of the policy will depend upon the organization's strengths and weaknesses and, to some degree, the personalities involved. As the issues are addressed and as the emotions of those involved begin to rise, it must be kept in mind that the critical issue must be the support of increased access to data process power. That power, in whatever form, must be available to those who can best use it to their advantage. Whatever the outcome, a strong, clear policy must be developed and once in place, everyone must be expected to adhere to that policy, regardless of their personal feelings.

One answer to these questions is the adoption of the Information Center concept. This is, by no means, a panacea. However, it does provide a number of distinct advantages. Properly installed and managed, actively promoted, the Information Center can provide distinct positive solutions to the problems which have been outlined in the preceding paragraphs.

The Information Center approach allows the use of large-scale data processing power to be made directly available to all clients who require that power. One of the difficulties encountered with the use of personal computers in a business environment is that, while they do provide a great deal of power for the price, that power and particularly the storage needed are often not sufficient to accommodate the work people want to do once they become comfortable with the equipment. The Information Center can, at least in theory, provide unlimited processing power.

The questions of control, of hardware expense, programs, and data can be more adequately administered through the joint efforts of the clients and the MIS department. A primary concern must be the issue of control of the organization's data. The MIS department, as a result of years of experience in this area, can install appropriate safeguards which will assure the data can be reproduced if it becomes necessary to do so. Instances of the destruction of considerable amounts of data in personal computers because of some error, and then not being able to recreate that data, or to be able to do so only with a great deal of effort, are not unknown.

Redundancy of data can also be limited. That data which is captured on the data center hardware can be used as a part of the Information Center. This means that data, if it is already available on the system, does not have to be rekeyed in order to be used. This can represent considerable savings in both time and money, particularly as the use of direct data processing expands.

Redundant programs are also an issue which is often ignored in the rush to install a personal computer in every department or section of an organization. The long-range implications here can pose serious potential difficulty for those organizations which allow the installation of such computers in an uncontrolled manner. As an example, assume a manufacturing organization which has several factories producing identical, or at least similar, products at three different locations. Assume that each of these factories face the same two major problems, the scrap rate is too high and the control and follow-up of preventative maintenance of the factory equipment is a manual, time-consuming effort which, because it is so cumbersome, is not being done in an adequate fashion.

It is not inconceivable that, in the absence of any policy and any acceptable alternatives from the MIS department, each plant manager, viewing these problems as significant, will purchase a personal computer and devise his own solution to these problems. In this situation, the organization will have six separate solutions to these two basic problems. Using the Information Center approach, a single solution can be developed for each problem and then implemented (copied) in each of the plants.

Using this method, not only has the effort to control these problems been reduced by a factor of three, but there will now be a single, common system for each of the factories. Not only will everyone be handling scrap and preventive maintenance in the same manner, but when improvements or changes to the system are required, the changes can be installed in all locations. This represents a considerable saving in both time and money.

There is an ancillary benefit to the preceding example. When problems arise in one factory with either of the systems, a check with one of the other locations can determine if anything has gone wrong there; if the answer is yes, it may be a program or data problem, if not, the cause must be due to some other factor. This can be an important consideration in attempting to isolate and correct problems.

There is another benefit to the development of systems under the Information Center approach, particularly where one program will be used in several locations. Adequate documentation can be developed as a part of each system and can then be distributed with the programs. This is more important than may be apparent. The documentation will greatly improve the ability of each location to operate the system in the event of changes in personnel. When using the personal computer approach, documentation will not be the same at each location.

The importance of documentation must not be overlooked. The record of the typical MIS department, as it concerns documentation, is poor.

Unless emphasis is placed on documentation, in either the Information Center or using personal computers, this serious problem will only grow worse. The potential to improve the control of documentation is much better under the Information Center than through using personal computers. While the typical MIS department fails in its documentation effort, usually someone else in the MIS department with an understanding of the particular system and programming knowledge, can overcome the problems. This may not be so easy where personal computers are used; no one else may have any understanding about the system, and if an esoteric programming language such as Fortran has been used, deciphering the code can be almost impossible.

An additional benefit of the Information Center is the ability to use large-scale data processing hardware and the new "higher level" programming languages to "snowplow" many of the more common MIS problems. Where, in the past, concern has focused, necessarily, on the most cost-effective methods to utilize (because of high hardware costs) the data processing equipment, the changing people/hardware expense ratio has made the Information Center practical.

This changing relationship is quite apparent. Several years ago, the typical MIS installation had a budget breakdown which allocated approximately thirty percent to people and forty-five to fifty-five percent to hardware. The declining cost of hardware, the increasing cost of people (particularly systems and programming people), coupled with the growing numbers of people required to handle the increased demands for new MIS projects have shifted this ratio to something closer to thirty percent for hardware and fifty percent for people.

Many organizations, even in the face of the increasing expense of systems and programming people and the difficulties inherent in finding and retaining such people, have continued to build their systems and programming staffs at a rapid pace. Data processing people, particularly well-qualified data processing people are, and will continue to be, in great demand. The turnover rate among these people averages more than twenty-five percent per year. Excessive amounts of time, money, and energy are expended in the continuing process of locating, training, and replacing these people.

Clearly, this circumstance cannot be allowed to continue; too much valuable time and energy are lost in such a process. Projects fall behind, morale slips, and MIS continues to be viewed as delivering a less than desirable service. The Information Center provides a viable approach which can help mitigate some of these concerns.

How can the Information Center provide help with a problem such as the shortage of data processing personnel? The principal tenet of the

Information Center is to place more of the work done by MIS in the hands of those who need the systems, the MIS clients. Any work which can be done by these clients (and this can be a considerable amount of work) lessens the demands on the MIS department. The introduction of a new type of programming language has made this a practical approach.

These new programming languages are usually referred to as "Fourth Generation" or "High-Level Programming" languages. They are written in such a manner that the programming is done in English, as opposed to some of the exotic technical languages such as Cobol now in widespread use. Any of these languages can be mastered by people without any prior technical training or knowledge in a very short time. It will take some effort and patience to become proficient in the use of these languages, but the effort is much less than usually believed.

If the use of these programming languages is accepted by the members of the client departments, if they are willing to learn how to use them, and if they will indeed use them to attack some of the data processing problems they now face, great, in many instances dramatic, progress can be attained. This is a common situation in all organizations to which the Information Center effort can be applied with positive results.

While most organizations are painfully aware of their large MIS project backlogs, which are often in excess of three years, and while the Information Center can be used to relieve some of this backlog, there is another backlog in existence which should also be addressed and which can be addressed very effectively through the Information Center. This backlog might be referred to as the "unadmitted" backlog.

The unadmitted backlog is made up of those potential projects which clients feel they need or which they know would be most helpful. Because the common situation is that the organization already has a large MIS project backlog, most clients are aware these projects will not receive any attention and they view, probably correctly, any attempt to focus meaningful attention on these projects as futile. Many of these projects tend to be limited in scope, both as to size and the impact on more than one section or department. Because they usually affect only one client, they are ideal candidates for development under the Information Center approach.

The effective operation of the Information Center must be predicated upon the ability to provide sufficient processing power. This must be done so that consistently fast terminal response time is available to all clients. Obviously, in order to accomplish this, adequate data processing power must be available. The data center operating environment must also be stable. Slow terminal response times or loss of the entire system will quickly cause frustration among the clients. While it is impossible to totally eliminate these types of problems, today's data processing hardware can, if the operating systems are properly structured, provide almost trouble-free performance and consistently fast response times. The cost of this hardware, in relation to the results and client satisfaction obtained, should be considered minimal.

These issues, system availability, consistently fast terminal response times, and programming languages which are easily mastered by nontechnical people, are the key elements to a successful Information Center. Attempts to install an Information Center service, while withholding any of these elements will, if not guarantee, certainly enhance the propensity for failure of the project. The costs and risks associated with the venture must be clearly understood by the organization's senior management, and a firm agreement to support the effort must be obtained from that group.

The selection of the programming languages which will be offered will, in most cases, grow through an evolutional process. There are any number of programming packages available (and the list is growing rapidly) which are easy to learn without any prior technical training or knowledge. Many of these packages provide very explicit computer based tutorial or *help* facilities which allows the client to learn the language and features of the system at his own speed. Anyone with an interest and the willingness to apply themselves can become quite proficient and comfortable with the system and the language in a very short time. An additional advantage is that this can be accomplished with minimal assistance from technical people. These "high level" languages do offer true "do-it-yourself" capabilities.

The essence of the Information Center must be to create an environment where people outside the MIS department can, through a reasonable application of their own effort, achieve significant progress in helping themselves make effective and practical use of the organization's large-scale data processing hardware. The key to this function is the ability of the clients to solve a certain spectrum of their own data processing problems on their own time and at their own pace.

The connotation of the *certain spectrum* of problems is important. This is true from two perspectives. First, the clients must understand that large systems, which have significant impact within the organization or which are of a complex nature, will continue to be developed within the MIS department. The other aspect is to make certain this same message is delivered to the members of the systems and programming departments of the organization.

As the Information Center is introduced, substantial resistance to the effort can be anticipated to develop within the MIS department. Many members of the department will assume that the Information Center signals the demise of their efforts within the organization. What will occur is that much of what MIS people currently feel is mundane, routine work, can be transferred to the client departments. This will increase the MIS effort without increasing the MIS head count, a subject of justifiable concern in many organizations.

The Information Center presents real benefits for all concerned. The clients can make progress with some of their data processing problems, and the members of the MIS department will be able to apply their talents and skills to more interesting, challenging, and productive tasks.

How can an organization implement an Information Center? As is the case with any new project within an organization, the Information Center must have a champion; someone who believes in the concept, who understands both the potential and pitfalls of the concept, and who will, when necessary, fight to see the project reach its goals.

While the drive for the installation of the Information Center can conceivably originate anywhere within the organization, the ideal situation is when the leadership originates in the MIS department. The combination of technical skills and knowledge, in addition to the knowledge of the work being done or required by the MIS clients, places the MIS manager in a strong position to lead the effort. Wherever the initiative originates, it is imperative that senior management not only concur, but also agree to actively support the effort.

It may occur that the management of the MIS department will view the Information Center as a threat to their power, much the same way as they view the personal computer as a threat. Such a stance is unfortunate. The concept of providing increased computing power to the clients, whether by personal computer or through the Information Center is valid; it will occur; it is occurring. Efforts to delay or stop the process means everyone involved, the MIS clients, and the entire organization will lose time and momentum. Attempting to delay the process is simply an attempt to "hold back the dawn," it will not work.

By whatever means necessary, MIS must be involved. The planning for the required hardware, the creation of the appropriate operating environment, assistance with the investigation and selection of the programming languages to be used by the clients, technical assistance, and the coordination and control of the function as it grows will require considerable MIS involvement. If the current management of the MIS department is not pushing the Information Center concept, they should be encouraged to do so; if they resist the installation of the process, they should be replaced.

What are some of the considerations for the introduction and successful implementation of the Information Center? Because this discussion is nontechnical and because specific technical considerations, such as type and size of equipment used, operating systems, and specific programming languages offered, will vary from organization to organization, it will be assumed for purposes of this discussion, that those questions have been resolved. The Information Center considerations discussed here then, will be of a general nature.

Assuming the technical considerations whatever they may be, have been resolved, the effort should begin with a sales/marketing emphasis. First it is necessary to conduct a survey of the potential market for the Information Center with the organization. This is where the assistance of MIS will prove beneficial, not from a pure sales/marketing approach, the track record of most MIS people in this area is abominable, but to help identify the potential systems which can be developed using the Information Center. Once the initial inertia of the project is overcome, identification of potential systems will not be a problem; more will appear than can be handled, but the effort is necessary in the beginning.

The survey should address questions such as, who (which clients) would react favorably to the use of the Information Center? What are some of the potential applications in that client's department? After identifying several clients who would be willing to cooperate and who have appropriate applications, the next step is to further identify members of that group who will provide enthusiastic support for the concept and be willing to put forth the effort to make the projects successful. These questions, particularly with the assistance of MIS, can be answered very quickly in most organizations. There are always a number of clients who have unfilled needs, who can, often with little encouragement, provide a "grocery list" of potential projects.

The selection of the clients to approach to begin the Information Center is entirely a function of personality. Select those who have an interest in the project, who have the patience to learn the system, and, if possible, those who have some technical training. Many people have personal computers in their homes; if someone can be found in the organization who has a personal computer and has a potential project, they would be an ideal candidate for a pilot project.

Once several clients who have potential projects and who are amenable to becoming active participants in the process have been identified, the Information Center pilot projects can begin. The selection of the participants and the projects in the pilot process must be done with great care. It is of paramount importance that these first efforts be successful. Not only will success encourage others to join the Information Center process, but it will increase MIS credibility.

The projects selected for the pilot phase should be those which are not overly complex, but which will produce meaningful results. One area which will provide ample ground for pilot projects is the automation of accounting spread sheets. Most organizations have any number of jobs which are done by hand each month, which are for the most part, a routine copying of information, the placement of figures and the adding of columns and crossfooting of totals. This is often a tiresome, redundant effort. This type of work can be very easily accommodated by several of the available high-level programming languages.

There are several benefits to the selection of projects of this type for the pilot process. The programming is very straightforward and can be easily mastered by those with no prior experience. The results, in terms of reduction in the manual effort, once the programming is completed, can be dramatic, savings of as much as seventy-five percent of the former effort are common. This type of project satisfies several of the basic pilot criteria, ease of programming and implementation and a demonstrable benefit to the clients.

Through the pilot process, whatever assistance is required from the MIS department must be provided. As much "hand holding" as is required to make the pilot projects successful must be available. The goal here must be to develop the pilot projects in the shortest, most friction-free manner possible. It may be, in order to realize this goal, MIS will have to provide most of the programming skill and do the documentation. The pilot project must demonstrate the practicality of the process and develop concrete examples of the work which can be accomplished. These successful results will then be used as a part of the sales/marketing campaign; therefore, whatever MIS has to do to move the pilot phase along must be done.

The effort to introduce the Information Center to the organization should be approached in a professional manner. A well-planned, carefully prepared and professionally delivered presentation which describes the Information Center, which explains the reasons for its implementation, and provides examples of the work which has been done (through the pilot projects), and also the work which can be done, will set the process in motion in a positive manner.

Time and effort must be devoted to the presentation in order to allay fears of all concerned with regard to the process and to how they will be affected by these changes in their work environments. It must be explained that the Information Center is not being installed to replace people with machines, as it is not, but, to increase productivity, make the work being done more interesting and challenging, and to help reduce much of the difficult, tedious work now being done. It should also be explained, as carefully as possible, that regardless of personal feelings, the use of computers will increase, that people who do not develop the required skills will, in time, find themselves and their skills outmoded.

Attention should be paid to the mechanics of the presentation. If possible, color slides should be used rather than overhead foils. Not only are slides more professional and dramatic than the overhead foils usually used for in-house presentations, but the fact that slides, rather than foils are being used, will in itself have a dramatic effect. Often in-house help can be obtained to produce these slides and the cost can be very small. The use of slides gives the presentation a polished effect.

Obviously the delivery of the presentation is just as important as its preparation. Adequate time must be put into the rehearsal so that the delivery will be crisp and to the point. The use of slides will eliminate the requirement for the use of a prepared text; this in itself can improve the presentation because of the usual tendency to simply read a prepared text which is often less than satisfactory.

Because the primary audience for the Information Center presentation will not possess a data processing orientation and in most cases will have little actual data processing experience, the presentation must be as jargon-free as possible. The idea is to instruct these groups about the potential advantages the Information Center can bring to their particular areas. The goal must be to convey the message to these clients in a manner to which they can relate with ease. Not only must the use of jargon be avoided, but also any tendency to talk down to the audience must also be avoided. The presentation must deliver the Information Center message in a business-like manner.

Correctly prepared and properly delivered, the Information Center presentation will elicit sufficient interest and enthusiasm so that in a short time the problem will shift from that of attempting to interest clients, to the concern of coordination and control of the effort. Once they understand what can be accomplished, and see how easily those results can be realized, the clients will want to begin to attack the unadmitted project backlog. This situation should be thought out ahead of time and appropriate planning must be in place to satisfy these demands.

Obviously, if the Information Center is to be successful, some ongoing technical help must be provided by the MIS department; this is the reason why it is important for the MIS department to be heavily involved in the process, and why it will be much more likely to succeed if MIS is involved. The question is, "After the pilot projects have been completed, how much technical assistance should MIS provide?"

The assistance provided by MIS will vary from organization to organization. The level of support can range from minimal, as an example, where the MIS involvement is limited to providing the hardware resource, the programming languages, and training manuals and nothing more, to a situation where someone from MIS provides everything required to implement a system, which would include programming and documentation.

While the MIS involvement range can cover a broad spectrum, the premise of the Information Center is to allow the clients to solve many of their own data processing related problems without heavy MIS involvement. When the MIS level of involvement rises much above that of minimal, many of the benefits of the Information Center will be lost.

One key to the success of the Information Center is that it be client driven. Those clients who are not willing to take a reasonable amount of initiative and to make progress on their own probably do not have an adequate commitment. Time and effort expended attempting to encourage, or force, these clients to continue with the effort will only direct resources from more deserving clients. Those who do not appropriately respond, should be abandoned. Once underway, the Information Center will produce more active and willing clients than can be comfortably accommodated; time spent with laggards is essentially time wasted.

As the Information Center gains prominence and as more clients join the effort, there will be attempts to begin rather more grandiose projects. In the beginning this should be avoided. The difficulty here is that the risk of failure with these projects, at least in the early stages, will not be offset by the potential payoffs if successful. Most clients, although they may not realize it, will still be in the preliminary stage of the effort, they will require more experience before they attempt a large, complex project. There will be a plethora of small projects which should be pursued in order to gain experience and confidence.

The process used in the development of systems under the Information Center is, if it is to be effective, much different than the conventional data processing approach. In the usual data processing approach to the development of a new system, a great deal of time and attention must be paid to the analysis and design of the system before any programming is attempted. In this environment, it is critical that as much as practical be known about the system prior to beginning the programming.

In developing systems under the Information Center, a different approach can be taken, which will allow for much more rapid development and which will usually be viewed as a very positive factor by those in the client departments. This method is often referred to as the heuristic, or trial-and-error approach.

Ideally, the person developing the system under the heuristic approach is the person most familiar with the work being done and the results to be expected from the system. This knowledge, combined with the direct access to the computing hardware and the ease of programming, mean the client can afford to develop and program the system in an interactive manner. The programming is done on the CRT, including the development of the reports. As the work progresses, changes, as they become appropriate, can be quickly and easily made.

The great appeal to the clients in this approach can be found in several areas. First the clients, doing everything themselves, do not have to wait for MIS. They are usually impressed by the lack of the usual MIS "red tape and control" which, while very necessary for large MIS projects, is often viewed by the clients as an unnecessary encumbrance.

Results, because everything is done interactively, are rapid. The client can see instantly the result of the work being done, if it is not what is desired it can be changed "on the fly." The current high client level of frustration with the MIS delays to help solve their problems will, in the case of the Information Center systems, be eliminated.

Documentation, a subject which is currently ignored within many MIS installations, can be as complete and detailed as the client desires, since they will be doing that work themselves. This is an area where the management of the client areas must use caution. Documentation is an important aspect of any data processing work and it should not be ignored. The client manager must remain aware that, in the Information Center environment, the documentation is the client's responsibility, if it is inadequate or nonexistent MIS will not be able to provide assistance.

The question of control cannot be completely ignored in the Information Center environment. As the work being done grows, there must be some method which can provide communication about what is being done in various areas of the organization. The preceding example of the independent use of personal computers at three factory sites to develop redundant systems applies to the Information Center if methods are not used to monitor activities.

An effective method to provide the needed communication is through the establishment of an Information Center *clients group*. Whoever leads the Information Center effort should assume the responsibility to establish this group. Regular meetings among the clients will provide a forum to discuss problems and new techniques. These client meetings allow those involved in the Information Center effort to help each other, and to strengthen their own knowledge and confidence at the same time.

As an adjunct to the client group, an Information Center newsletter should also be published on a regular basis. The content of the newsletter should cover new systems being developed, new programming language being considered for use in the Information Center, and any new processes which have been discussed which can help clients with their work. Client questions and criticisms should be solicited and addressed in the newsletter.

The use of the client group and the newsletter will, in addition to furthering the work being done in the Information Center, also help those with overall responsibility monitor that which is being done and when necessary they can channel this effort in order to avoid redundant or unnecessary work.

There is an ancillary benefit to the formation of the Information Center client group, which can prove of great benefit to whoever leads the effort. It can be an effective method of developing a high level of knowledge of what is being done throughout the entire organization. The interaction provided in the Information Center can expand the knowledge of those charged with the responsibility for its success.

While there are a number of very positive aspects to the Information Center, there are also some distinct pitfalls which must be watched for and avoided where possible. One of the common problems will be the difficulty of the clients to find time to develop the systems under the Information Center. There is an irony here, because this is just the difficulty MIS faces in attempting to fulfill its mission. This situation is really related to the degree of commitment on the part of the client. Those who possess sufficient desire will find the time to make progress.

The failure to accurately judge the level of demand placed upon the system, and to provide adequate resources to accommodate that demand, can produce a most deleterious effect on the Information Center effort. Using the hardware to "snowplow" MIS concerns is a valid concept, but only if the hardware level is sufficient to support what will be a growing demand. Again, this is one of the reasons for solid senior management support.

Someone, preferably in the MIS department, must be assigned responsibility for remaining aware of the developing trends in the technology as it pertains to the Information Center. Advances in data processing technology and techniques are in a constant state of change; today's "leading edge" soon becomes obsolete; it is important that the organization remains informed of what is available and is positioned to take advantage of those technical developments which are appropriate for the continued success of the Information Center.

What does all this mean for the future? The dramatic reductions in cost of hardware, across the broad spectrum not just large-scale hardware, the increasing ease of use and the growing demand for the results which can be produced, mandate a continued explosive growth in this area.

The effects of high-level languages show, beyond any doubt, that in many instances the work of writing and testing programs can be reduced by as much as eighty percent and that this work can, with some rather limited training, be done by people with little programming knowledge.

This means, simply, that a great deal of the complex data processing work being done today by MIS can be shifted to the client areas. As this occurs, there will be a concomitant shift of the mission of the MIS department. The concept of a "Computer Utility," where the processing power is supplied directly to the clients, so they can do much of their own work, will become commonplace.

The analogy between the computer utility and the electric utility is sound. Just as we do not particularly care how our electric power is delivered, that is on wire on poles or underground, and we do not care what problem the power company may have in providing us power, all we want is light when we turn on the switch, the same will occur with the computer utility. The clients will not care, probably in most instances not even know, what equipment is located in the data center, or what operating system is being used; all they want is to have processing power available when they need it.

What does this mean for MIS? Does it mean the demise of the MIS function? No! The MIS effort will become more specialized, more technical, and even more critical. Large systems will still require heavy MIS support, although in well-run organizations, most new systems will be purchased software packages, rather than in-house designed. The increasing use of Data Base Management Systems will require increased MIS support on a technical and analytical level.

The issues of coordination of the work being done and the control of the organizations data are issues which will require strong MIS involvement and support. In short, there will be plenty for MIS to do. The MIS department should be able to shed some of its mundane functions and be able to concentrate on a much more challenging array of opportunities.

As the use of higher level programming languages grows, particularly in conjunction with the use of Data Base Management Systems, we will see the concept of the "disposable program" evolve. If a person with limited experience can produce a program in fifteen man hours which currently requires perhaps eighty man hours using Cobal (and it can be done today), the current problem with large MIS maintenance backlogs can be effectively attacked. This means we will not attempt to enhance these Cobol programs; we will simply rewrite the entire program in a high-level language and throw the Cobol program away. The day of the disposable program draws near!

None of the ideas or statements in this chapter are theoretical, in fact, most of them are not new; they are being used in a small number of "leading edge" installations today. They do work, they are effective, and they are not difficult to cost justify.

Those organizations which adopt a well-planned, organized, concerted effort to move to an Information Center and which see the effort through to completion will not only greatly improve the effective utilization of the data processing resources within the organization, but they will also enhance their competive edge in a number of ways. Conversely, those organizations which choose to ignore the potential of the Information Center will find themselves in a reactive, catch-up mode which may cause them real harm.

Chapter VIII
Project Management within the Management Information Services Department

The overall success record of the typical Management Information Services department with regard to the development of new information systems, or the conversion and enhancement of existing systems, has often been less than adequate. Most (probably all) organizations, have experienced difficulty with these projects; many have endured significant turmoil in their attempts to develop and install projects of any size.

These experiences cover a broad spectrum of problems. Included are situations such as projects which are not completed within budget (both time and expense) limitations. Systems which, once completed, do not deliver that which had been originally proposed. Systems which, when implemented, proved to be far more costly or difficult to operate than had been originally promised. Or, systems which have proved to be difficult, if not impossible, to change in order to accommodate new requirements.

While the preceding circumstances are rather common, there is a worse situation which, on occasion, occurs. That situation is the abandonment of a particular project after a considerable amount of effort and expense have been devoted to the effort. This situation presents a particular tragedy, not only because of the lost time, effort, and money; but perhaps more importantly, because it is a circumstance which can, in all instances, be avoided.

The avoidance of such unfortunate circumstances rests with appropriate management and control of MIS projects. Properly managed, these projects can be delivered on time, within budget, and in a fashion which will assure adherence to the original requirements of the project. This can be accomplished every time and with projects of any size, if appropriate project management techniques are in place and are followed.

A rather common rationale offered by MIS management when faced with project difficulty or failure, is to ascribe the cause of that failure to issues such as the complexity of the technology, inadequate equipment resources, or the lack of client or senior management support for the effort. While any of these items may indeed be valid reasons for project failure, there is always an underlying cause. That cause is the failure of the organization's MIS management to properly structure, control, and manage MIS projects.

The project development success rate and the degree of MIS client satisfaction can be greatly enhanced in any organization through the development of sound project management techniques, coupled with the continuing commitment to enforce the required project discipline. A discussion of those techniques and the concomitant disciplines will provide sufficient material to change the project development climate in any organization.

It must be remembered, however, that unless MIS management, with the concurrence and support of the organization's senior management, is willing to maintain the required resolve to enforce this structure and control, the desired results will not be forthcoming. It is not uncommon to find organizations which have put considerable effort and expense into this area but have not been willing to enforce the discipline. The result, of course, is failure. When this occurs, the feeling is usually that the process is at fault. That is incorrect; the process, properly installed and managed, works very well.

The consideration of support for the process transcends the MIS department. Because those outside the MIS department who are involved in the project will often fail to recognize the value of this controlled approach, they will often attempt to circumvent the process. The argument will run that the process is too time consuming, too cumbersome. The client will often maintain that all they need is a "simple" system. Pressure to eliminate parts of the process for a particular project must be resisted by MIS management. The only way MIS can prevail in such a situation is to seek the support of senior management. Without that support, the project will in most instances be, if not a failure, less than what it could have been.

Prior to a discussion of the mechanics of improved project management, it will be worthwhile to consider the criteria which should be used to judge the success of an MIS project. An understanding of this criteria is important, because it will provide a basis for a quality standard for project performance. If it is understood and agreed that each project will meet certain performance levels, the finished project can then be objectively judged against that criteria.

Adherence to the originally scheduled project time and expense deadlines is only one of the factors to be considered. Client satisfaction (does the project perform to the original requirements), operational performance (the lack of a heavy requirement to change the system or to apply extensive system enhancements), system flexibility (the ability to easily change the system if external conditions require such changes), and the actual operational costs, compared to the original estimated operational costs, are all factors which play a part in the determination of the final quality of the project.

These are not vague items which should be viewed as desirable; they are achievable results which should be the eventual goal of each project effort. While it may not be possible to completely achieve each of these specific goals in every project, careful project management will produce improving project quality which will, given time, overcome many of the current MIS development problems found in most organizations.

During the past few years, considerable improvement has been made in both the understanding of the processes required to improve the development of MIS projects and in the technical tools, particularly both operational and application software, available to produce much improved project results. The acceptance and use of these techniques, in conjunction with strong management control, are the key to improved organizational satisfaction with the Management Information Services department's products.

In those organizations where an appropriate commitment has been made to the subject of MIS project management and where, once made, the commitment has been honored, a substantial improvement in result has been achieved. Success rests with the willingness of the management of the MIS department to introduce, support, and when necessary, fight for, these concepts.

This effort may, in fact it probably will, prove to be a traumatic experience. The degree of trauma will depend upon the cultural climate within a particular installation. At a minimum, a certain degree of suspicion and discontent must be anticipated within the MIS department. Concern may very well arise in the client departments. This increased tension, coupled with a likely already low degree of MIS credibility, can make the effort on the part of MIS management substantial.

However, the benefits associated with the installation and use of improved project management techniques will more than offset the difficulty encountered. In any event, unless MIS and, where required, the organization's senior management are willing to demonstrate sufficient resolve in the issue, progress will not be made. One of the probable results of the imposition of these new processes will be the loss of MIS employees who will find themselves unable to tolerate the increased discipline. This circumstance must not be used as an excuse to abandon the effort; the existing problems in the MIS department will not be resolved without firm management action.

While MIS practitioners often consider themselves as "agents of change," it is often the case that when they must face change within their own environment, they tend to overreact. Whatever can be done to mitigate the effects of these changes, both within the MIS department and within the client departments, should be done; yet the process must continue to move ahead.

The specter of high rates of turnover of MIS employees haunts most data processing managers. The high demand and numerous opportunities encourage a great deal of personnel movement within the data processing industry. Because of this, some managers are reluctant to establish and enforce improved project development methods because they fear employee resistance and a resultant increase in turnover. This is really a case of "giving away the store." Sound personnel selection processes (hiring the right people to begin with), providing appropriate challenges and autonomy in a participative environment which encourages individual initiative and growth will, with time and patience, build a stable work force. The use of the Standard Project Management process, well-defined and fairly enforced, yet flexible enough to accommodate changes to the Standard Project Management system when they prove appropriate, will in the long run, help stabilize the environment.

Detail consideration of the processes and techniques used to manage information systems projects will provide insight into the steps which make up the process, and some of those areas which must be given careful consideration as the project moves from phase to phase in the development cycle.

The development of the MIS project, regardless of size, regardless of function (be it application system, such as, General Ledger or Accounts Receivable or an operational system such as the conversion to a new operating system or to a data base) must be considered as a series of well-defined steps which will provide, not only control through the entire development process, but also the ability to accurately monitor project progress. The monitoring of project progress must be carried on in a candid fashion, the goal is to be able to accurately determine the actual status of the project as it moves through the various project phases.

Candid project status reporting provides an early warning of potential difficulty and, if used appropriately, will eliminate the existence of "surprise" management situations. One of the genuine senior management concerns with the MIS project development process is the receipt of news

Project Management within the MIS Department 107

that, after reporting good progress for a considerable period of time, the project is suddenly far behind schedule.

There are only two reasons for such a circumstance to occur, either the project manager has been knowingly misleading senior management, a problem which no project management process, no matter how sophisticated, can eliminate, or the project manager has simply been unable to properly evaluate the actual status of the project, a situation which can be improved through the application of sound project management techniques. In the first instance, senior management should dismiss a project manager who is less than candid about the progress of the project. In the second, the introduction and use of the Standard Project Management system will stop the project "surprises."

The work associated with the process used to structure, manage, and control MIS projects, once developed, must become an integral part of the MIS department standards. This will provide a framework within which all MIS projects can be developed. Once the process has been developed and has been implemented via the department's standards, no deviation from the process should be allowed. This approach must become the department standard. The title SPM (Standard Project Management) is suggested as an appropriate name to apply to the concept.

The purpose of the Standard Project Management approach is simply to provide a consistent method which will assure that the same rules are applied to all MIS projects and that those rules are always followed. Standard Project Management provides consistency, control, and the opportunity to communicate the development process rules to anyone who becomes involved in a project. Standard Project Management, properly installed and used, is the catalyst to assure continued project success.

Prior to the consideration of the specific aspects of an MIS project, it is important to address a somewhat more subtle, yet important, component of project success. A salient consideration for any application project is to be absolutely clear with regard to the management of that project. Under no circumstances should the MIS department accept the responsibility for the ultimate management of an application project. It is the acceptance of this responsibility, either overt or covert, for such projects that has caused much of the difficulty encountered with projects in the past.

In any application project, although MIS must provide the technical assistance, and do much of the analytical work, the responsibility for the ultimate success or failure of that project must reside with the client department requesting the project. The first step with any project, once it has been approved for development by the appropriate organizational level of management, is to select a project manager. This person must be a member of the department which has requested the project. The appointment of the project manager should be made by the vice president responsible for that area where the project will be installed.

Until the project manager is appointed, MIS must refuse to begin any work of any kind on the project. This stance must be enforced regardless of the urgency or desirability of the project. This concept should be viewed as critical to project success. Too often, projects fail because they become through default, the province of MIS. Anytime this occurs, the results will usually be less than satisfactory. Unless the client clearly understands the extent of his involvement in the project and fully appreciates his responsibility, his commitment will not be total.

It is a common occurrence to find project situations where the client is "too busy" to devote the required time and attention to the project. This poses a dilemma for MIS, in that the project must move ahead. In order to keep the project moving, MIS will begin to make decisions which are the province of the client. Decisions about items such as data content, report layouts, and system controls will evolve in MIS through default. As the project deadline nears, as pressure mounts to finish the project grows, more of the critical decisions will be made by MIS without the complete involvement of the client.

At some point, either prior to implementation or at implementation itself, someone in the client department will begin to worry about the project details. When this occurs, problems will arise. The usual contention at this juncture is that while the project may indeed be sound from a technical point of view; it does not meet the requirements of the client.

Now changes, often massive changes, will be required to accommodate the client's needs. The results at this point are predictable. Increased tension between MIS and its client, project delays, revision of the project schedule, and general discontent. The lesson here should be clear; the client must assume overall responsibility for the project from the beginning and must retain that responsibility throughout the entire project cycle.

This approach of placing responsibility for the project on the client will probably be viewed as a difficult process. However, this is the only way in which MIS application projects should be handled. The reason is simple; the client always knows more about his requirements than the people in MIS; it is logical then that the primary responsibility for the project rest with the client.

What recourse does MIS have if, as the project moves ahead, the client fails to assert his project responsibility? MIS should not attempt to fill the void. Once it has been determined the client has stopped active management of the project, the MIS manager must bring that fact to the attention of the project manager's supervisor and also inform that person that, until active management of the project is resumed by the client, MIS will stop all work on that project.

It cannot be stressed too strongly, applications projects must be under the management of the appropriate client department. These are projects for these departments, their success or failure, beyond the obvious technical considerations, must rest with that management group.

If it is accurate to assume that the success of the development of applications projects rests with the management of those projects, how can this be accomplished? The primary consideration is to make certain that the Standard Project Management approach is indeed used for every project. This can be accomplished by linking the Standard Project Management effort to the MIS project development policies.

An MIS policy dealing with project development must be formulated and installed. That policy must be approved by the senior management of the organization. Once the policy is in place, a mechanism must be developed which will assure that all projects are handled in the same manner. This can be accomplished through providing documentation for the Standard Project Management process. In addition to detailing the duties and responsibilities of the client project manager and the MIS department representatives on the project team, this information should also explain the concept of the Standard Project Management process.

The Standard Project Management approach consists of the following items, which must be considered mandatory for the successful completion of any MIS project:

- Statement of Requirements
- General Specifications
- Detail Specifications
- The Testing Plan
- The Implementation Plan
- The Acceptance (Turnover) Phase

These components must be incorporated within the general framework of a process which assures that every project undergoes appropriate management control and that each phase receives the required approval through the various development stages. The purpose is to assure that, once approved, every project regardless of size or scope will be handled in exactly the same manner, and that the MIS standards will be followed.

The starting point for any MIS project is with the development of the Statement of Requirements. The function of the Statement of Requirements is to describe the content and scope of the proposed project. This document will describe that which is to be accomplished by the project, but it should also address those items which will be specifically omitted from the project. This pertains to items which would seem to be natural functions of such a project, but which will, for whatever reasons, be excluded.

It is an important facet of progress success that, in so far as practical, everyone understand what is to be included. In the absence of reference to the omission of specific items which could be assumed to be a normal part of the project, but which are not to be included, there is a danger that the client will assume those items will be included. When it becomes clear at some late stage of the project that these items are not included, difficulties are certain to arise. Either the clients will express their dissatisfaction, or worse yet, the project will have to be revised to include the missing items. Careful planning and communication in the specifications stage will alleviate much of this difficulty.

As an example, a project may be proposed to develop a single customer master file data base, which will replace several separate files now in use. However, for some reason, one of the existing files will continue to be used after the project is finished. This information should be spelled out in the Statement of Requirements, so there will be no doubt about what can be expected at the conclusion of the project.

The Statement of Requirements must address issues of project cost, both development and ongoing operational costs, the amount of effort (project manhours) required to complete the project, the estimated completion date of the project, and the anticipated degree of risk inherent in the project. This must be done in sufficient detail so as to provide a reasonably accurate appraisal of the effort required. Appropriate care must be put into this effort, while the Statement of Requirements may be viewed as an estimate by members of the project team, members of senior management will be asked to formally approve the plan and they will consider the Statement of Requirements a commitment to complete the project within the manpower hours and dollars shown in the specifications.

The question of the degree of project risk must not be overlooked. One of the difficulties encountered in MIS projects is the underestimation of the amount of effort, both technical and managerial, required to bring the project to completion. Too often the "Wonderful times 10,000" syndrome comes into play. Too much is promised, usually more than that which can be produced within the framework of the project.

The eagerness to use new technology, coupled with the desire of the client to move to a new system, will often obscure many of the potential project problems. Everyone will feel much can be accomplished, the problems will be minimized, the results overstated. Thus, there will emerge a feeling among the members of the project team that the project will not only be "Wonderful," it will be "Wonderful times 10,000."

The risks must be carefully considered, properly assessed, and factually presented as a part of the Statement of Requirements. Several items must be considered. The primary issue must be that of the technology of the project. Some questions must be asked, "Is this a new technology; has our staff any experience in this area? Will increased processing power be required, if so, what size increase, how much will it cost? Does the client departments staff understand the new concept, do they have sufficient department depth to make the system work?"

Consideration of the ability of the staff of the client department to understand and operate the system once it has been installed can be a critical issue. No matter how well-designed and programmed the system may be, if it is not properly used after it has been installed, or if it requires a lengthy training program before it operates correctly, the view of management will not be favorable.

Addressing these questions and doing the investigative work in a thorough manner will provide an informed appraisal of the risks inherent in each project. Once the degree of risk has been established, an estimate of the degree of risk can be included in the Statement of Requirements. This can be expressed in terms such as low, medium, or high, with regard to both the managerial and technical aspects of the project.

The discussion of the degree of risk is an important component of the Statement of Requirements. This provides those outside the project team, with limited if any technical knowledge, the opportunity to gain some perspective about the probability of success. In addition, if the assignment of the risk factor has been accurate, it can provide support for the project team should trouble occur. This is true because, if the factor has been designated as high, it will be reasonable to assume some additional difficulty will occur as the effort moves to completion.

It is an excellent idea, where practical, to limit the size of any individual project to a realistic size. It should be a matter of MIS policy to place a standard outside limit on the size of any development project. This need not imply that projects which exceed the limit should not be undertaken, but that larger projects should be broken down into manageable phases. Projects of excessive size present inherent problems which tend to exacerbate the difficulty of project management. Large projects never seem to come to a conclusion, people working on them must wait too long to see tangible results and they become frustrated. Many times, large projects require so much time to complete that, when completed, the original purpose of the project may no longer be valid in terms of the organization's then current objectives.

CHAPTER VIII

An important aspect of project phasing is to provide the opportunity to test the current direction of the project against the current requirements of the organization. As an example, assume a thirty-man year (ten people for three years) project to install an automatic branch office claims payment system for an insurance company. The project is not phased, but handled as one large single effort. Twenty-two months (twenty-two man years) later, a review of the project is held and it is found that it will now require an additional ten-man years, over the original estimate, to complete the project. It is also now apparent that some of the original requirements of the project, due to competitive factors, have changed. Now what? Should the project be scrapped and the effort written off? Should it be revised and restarted? Is the "sunk cost" considered so great that the project should be completed as originally planned even though it will not fully meet the new needs?

These situations do arise; phasing allows periodic reviews, not only to judge the quality of the work done, but also to provide the opportunity to accurately assess the direction of the project at that stage of its development. If adjustments do need to be made at the end of any phase, they can be made at a reasonable expense and the trauma will be reduced. A reasonable size for each phase of a project would be to set a limit in the area of six to eight thousand manhours for each phase.

If a phased approach is used to develop projects, each phase must be considered a separate project and all the steps which form the Standard Project Management process must be followed for each phase.

Once developed, the Statement of Requirements must be routed to the appropriate individuals within the organization for their formal approval. The size and scope of a particular project will determine the required level of approval. A dollar amount should be used as the basis for approval. In any event, the signatures of the MIS manager, the manager of the client department requesting the project, and their immediate superiors should be considered the minimum for any project.

There will be times, even in those organizations where an MIS steering committee is used to control projects and priorities, when pressure will mount to begin work on a project before the Statement of Requirements has been approved. In fact there will be instances where that pressure will be felt before the Statement of Requirements has been completed. These pressures must be resisted. If the project is so urgent, the pressure should be applied to the completion and approval of the Statement of Requirements, not to beginning the project.

Adopting such a position simply makes good sense. Until the Statement of Requirements has been approved by the required management levels, no one can be certain that the project proposed is the one which will be developed. Should the project scope be amended, or should the project be denied, any work done prior to approval will simply be lost.

The Statement of Requirements represents the "why" portion of the project design and implementation process. The effort here is to demonstrate why the particular project is important to the organization and why the investment in time and money should be devoted to this project rather than some other project. The Statement of Requirements must outline the projected return on investment of the project. Usually, this will be expressed in terms of dollars over a specific period of time. However, there will be occasions when the project cannot be cost justified on a strict return on investment basis, yet justification can be developed based on other facts, such as responding to actions of the organization's competition. Whatever the reason for the project, the anticipated return must be clearly identified.

While the Statement of Requirements represents the "why" portion of the project, the General and Detail Specifications phases of the project deal with the "how" aspects of the project. In these phases the project will be defined and the steps required to produce the finished product will be outlined.

The General Specifications phase of the development process deals with the broad outline of the project. This outline is developed from the information about the scope and function of the project as it was approved in the Statement of Requirements. This is the stage of the process where the representatives from MIS and the client department gather the information they will require in order to define the project in such a manner that the overall processes and functions of the system can be understood. The work done here will be in the area of processing functions, number of programs, types of processing, files affected, and general data flow.

Once the General Specifications have been developed, they should be presented for a design review session. The purpose of this review is to bring in people with knowledge of both the functions to be affected by the new system and members of MIS with knowledge of the current processing environment in order to carry out an in-depth review of the appropriateness of the system as it has been outlined in the General Specifications.

The review process intent should be to expose the system plan concept to those whose knowledge can provide assistance in the task of determining the practicality and probable effectiveness of the system once it is operational. These review sessions must be carried on in a spirit of attempting to provide positive assistance in the joint effort to develop the best possible system. The client project manager must control the review in such a manner that personalities or political differences are not allowed to cloud the effort to produce the best possible system.

CHAPTER VIII

As a practical matter, the issue of politics will have to be dealt with to various degrees, in all system development projects. Everyone involved in the process will attempt to protect their particular interests. This must be expected as a normal consequence of the development process, the use of a phased approach, with appropriate authorizations at the relevant points in the develoment will help mitigate some of these problems.

Because there is usually a time lag between the preparation of the General Specifications and their approval, preliminary work should begin on the Detail Specifications as soon as the General Specifications have been completed. This should not imply that the effort to gain approval for the General Specifications should be allowed to slacken, the push for that approval must continue. Because of the amount of work involved in the Detail Specifications phase, delay in that portion of the project will have a serious impact on the project schedule.

The purpose of the Detail Specification phase is to develop, in great detail, the various parts of the system. One of the functions of this phase is to develop the specifications which will be used to write the system programs. If the Detail Specification phase is properly managed, the work required to actually write the programs will be greatly reduced. One of the real difficulties encountered in the development of systems is the tendency to begin to write the programs before there is a clear understanding of what it is those programs are to accomplish.

When the Detail Specifications are poorly done, or, as sometimes happens, they are simply ignored, increased difficulty can be anticipated in the writing of the programs and in the attempt to test those programs. Much of the usual difficulty with project delays can be traced to the rewriting of program code. Well-done Detail Specifications will avoid that problem. No program coding should begin until the Detail Specifications have been approved.

The Detail Specifications must be subjected to the same review process as the General Specifications. However, the makeup of this review team will be of a more technical nature. The primary concern at this stage of development will be with the design of the system files, the programs to be used, the processing methods being considered, and the myriad other data processing aspects of the project. While nontechnical people who have an interest in the process should be invited to attend, the emphasis must be on the technical considerations.

It is often the case that the requirement for peer reviews of the work being done will meet with resistance from members of the project team. The ego factor will begin to come into play. There will be a tendency to take any suggestions or comments as personal criticisms. When this occurs it must be dealt with by the appropriate client and MIS managers. The concern must be to avoid dealing in personalities, yet to face design flaws and problems and to resolve them.

This effort is an excellent example of the "people" skills which are required to move projects toward successful completion. It is in dealing with issues of this type, and in their successful resolution, where the real "art" and "creativity" of project management come into play. The ability to deal effectively with people is one skill which should not be overlooked when selecting project leaders, whether from the MIS or the client departments.

The makeup of the project team will also have a direct effect upon the ultimate success or failure of the project. While it should be obvious that appropriate members of the system development section of the MIS department and of the client department which is requesting the project must be members of the team, it is often the case that other potentially important team members are overlooked. While too many participants may cause more delay than progress, other groups should be considered and where appropriate, asked to join the team.

If more than one department will have direct involvement in the system when it is operational, they should provide a member of the team, if not in a full-time capacity, at least on an advisory basis. As an example, a new marketing system may be approved for development. Because this new system will affect the work done in both the sales and accounting departments, these departments must also be aware of the work being done. Systems must not be developed in a vacuum, when that is allowed to happen difficulty is certain to arise.

One section which will be involved in every MIS system, yet which seldom receives appropriate attention in terms of early and continuing involvement, is the data center. Every project should, as a mandatory requirement, have a member of the data center staff as a project team member. This person must be assigned the responsibility for the assurance that the interests of the data center will be considered as the project moves ahead. Too often, the data center receives the finished project with little or no formal notification. One of the causes of delayed project implementation and ongoing operational problems is this "surprise" method of presenting projects to the data center.

The objective, when considering the selection of the project team members, must be to make certain that all sections of the organization which will be affected by the particular project will have an opportunity to be represented on the project team. Some of these members may be active for the full duration of the project, others for only a short time, or only on an informational basis, yet they should all be asked to participate. Positive action in this area will go a long way toward reduction of the we/they dichotomy often found in development projects.

The MIS policies and the Standard Project Management system must make appropriate provision for the deliverance of accurate system documentation. This is a key issue; one, which in far too many instances, is not accorded appropriate consideration. The requirements, as they pertain to documentation, must be quite explicit. Each phase of the project effort must contain a requirement for a certain amount of documentation; if that documentation has not been produced, the next phase of the project cannot begin. The use of control of this type is the only method which will assure that the required documentation will be produced.

Again, this approach will cause unrest within MIS. People will want to ignore the question of documentation, to put it off so they can concentrate on the really "important" aspects of the project. This cannot be tolerated. Clear, easily updated system documentation, including client and data center documentation, must be produced. The long-term serviceability of the system will be contingent upon the quality of the system documentation; it must not be given perfunctory support.

The three final aspects of the development of the system, testing, implementation, and acceptance must be given particular attention. There is often a feeling that, once the programs have been written and tested, the "real" work of the project has been accomplished and little attention needs to be devoted to the remaining work. Nothing could be more incorrect. The proper management and control of these aspects of the project are as important as any other.

System testing, in its simplest context, is the process of thoroughly testing out all the programs which make up the system. First, the programs should be individually tested to ascertain that they are operating as they have been designed to operate and that they handle the data being passed to them in the correct manner. When the programs do indeed operate in the individual mode, they must be tested as integral subsets of the entire system. Unfortunately, this aspect of the testing process is often not done in a very careful manner. The result is that, once operational, the system encounters inordinate difficulty which results in an excessive number of system reruns in order to finally make it work correctly. These problems should be discovered in the testing phase of the project. Of course, the effort required to do this may be considerable and the work may delay the implementation of the system, yet the result will be greater client satisfaction.

The goal of system testing is to run the system, using adequate volumes of actual data as input, so as to parallel the operational conditions under which the system will function in the production environment. The testing should begin with small, selected assortments of input data and, as they are successfully processed, the volume and complexity of the data should be increased.

It is impossible to attempt to carry out testing which will cover one hundred percent of the conditions likely to be found in the production environment. There are simply too many combinations in the typical system to recreate them in a test environment. The goal should be to build test conditions which will cover the bulk of the expected situations and to assure that, given those situations, the individual programs and the entire system operate as desired.

Once the MIS systems and programming section has assured itself that the system testing has been accomplished in a successful manner, the system should be "turned over" to the client department and the data center for the implementation phase of the project. This is a critical step! The client and the data center staff members will now attempt to use the system without help from the systems and programming section. This is the production mode of the system.

The thrust in this phase of the project, is to determine the validity of the system design and the adequacy of the operational documentation. Because the appropriate members of the data center and the client departments will have been active throughout the project process, they will have a great deal of familiarity with the system; therefore, they should be able to carry out the implementation process with little difficulty.

It should be anticipated, however, that rather minor problems will arise. This is why the implementation procedure is used, to identify and correct these problems in the early stages of the implementation. While the implementation phase may be carried out as a part of actual production processing, it is better for all involved if this is done as either a test situation, or as a parallel to a production run. The number of implementation runs should depend upon the results obtained by the implementation team as they test the system.

The more involved and familar the implementation team members are with the system, the less time and effort will be required to carry out the implementation phase. A number of the questions and concerns which would normally arise in the course of the implementation process will have been resolved as a result of the prior involvement of these people.

The acceptance of the system by the client and the data center staff from the project team should be done on a formal basis. The significance of this process is that the client and data center teams agree that the system operates correctly and that it can be successfully operated without the intervention of members of the system and programming staff. The formal sign off signifies that the client and the data center can, unless unusual circumstances arise, operate the system without help from the development group. This will allow the development group to move on to new projects.

The issue of quality assurance, as it applies to the development of MIS projects, has begun to gain attention. The introduction and use of the Standard Project Management system approach, with its controls, peer reviews, and phased segments, focuses on the quality of the project, not only at each phase, but as a complete entity.

The use of the implementation and acceptance phases, on a formal basis, provide ample opportunity for the project clients and the data center to examine the product and to determine the quality of that product. As the use of the Standard Project Management process grows within the organization, it will become increasingly apparent that, unless a certain quality standard (the criteria outlined in the policy statement) is achieved, the project will not be accepted. It will take a while to make this happen, perhaps a long time in organizations where little or no discipline exists today, but it can be accomplished. With the proper diligence it will be found that project quality assurance will become an ancillary benefit of the Standard Project Management process.

If, as has been suggested, the criteria by which the completed projects are to be judged has been developed and published, continued use of the Standard Project Management process and the comparison of the completed development project against that criteria will provide a quality standard which will, with continuing effort, produce tangible improvements in project quality. With time, the achievement of the desired high quality level of MIS development projects can become almost automatic.

The use of the Standard Project Management process provides the basic structure to accurately understand the status of the project as it moves through the various development phases. This should be considered a critical feature of the Standard Project Management process. The breaking of the project into phases provides a series of checkpoints which must be used to gauge actual development progress against the original schedule. At each checkpoint one of three conditions will exist: the project will be on schedule, it will be ahead of schedule or, the project will be behind schedule.

If the project is on or ahead of schedule, nothing needs to be done except to keep on with the project. The concern must be with the project which is behind schedule. When this occurs, corrective action must be taken. First, the status of the project must be announced to the appropriate management group. It is important that when this announcement is made, a plan to put the project back on schedule must also be presented. It may be, after an analysis of the situation, that the only viable alternative is to extend the completion date of the project, if this is the case, so be it.

The paramount consideration must be that once the project is deemed to be behind schedule that fact must be made known. While the Standard Project Management process will provide the information about the status of the project, making that information public is the responsibility of the managers of the project. If the problems encountered are made known early enough, if the reasons for the delay are valid, and if there is a plan in effect which will resolve the problem as well as can be expected, the clients and senior management will usually adopt an understanding attitude. Hiding the facts, denying that the project will be late or over budget (a circumstance often encountered with MIS projects), will in the long run, do no one any good.

No process, no matter how accurate, can force those involved in the development project to admit they are in trouble. The prime consideration is the ability of the project managers to accept responsibility for the difficulty; if they are unwilling to do so, the prior system delays, excuses, and finger pointing will continue.

This chapter has addressed the problems inherent in the management of large MIS development projects, which would include the installation of software packages as well as in-house developed projects. The ideas presented are not new nor are they esoteric. They are simply aspects of sound management applied to the MIS function. These are logical steps, which if followed, will ensure a much greater degree of project success and client satisfaction than is currently the case in most organizations.

This process outlines a managerial approach to the development and implementation of MIS projects. In the past, most MIS projects have been developed from a technical, rather than a management basis. That is, the emphasis has been on the equipment, the software and the programming, and analysis. Inadequate attention has been paid to the overall management of the project, of the placement of appropriate responsibility (and authority), and the discipline required to carry this out. There is ample evidence to demonstrate that extensive focus on the technical aspects to the exclusion of the managerial, does not work. Almost any organization which has implemented MIS development projects can attest to this fact.

However, the same errors are repeated! Until an approach such as the Standard Project Management system is installed and used, no improvement in the development of projects can be expected. The imposition of such a process will generate a certain amount of resistance. Clients, members of the MIS department, and perhaps members of senior management will view the process as too confining, too cumbersome, as creating too much "red tape."

While it is correct that in most organizations the introduction of the Standard Project Management process will require cultural changes, both in MIS and in the client departments, these changes, and the subsequent results, will prove to be worth the effort. Many times the attempt to move to an improved environment fails because management does not stand firm. Too much is at stake, for the entire organization, not to make Standard Project Management work!

CHAPTER IX
The MIS Steering Committee

Many successful MIS installations have been guided to that success through a commitment to the principle that the MIS function bears a great similarity to a separate business, in reality a smaller, complete business within the larger organization. Because MIS does indeed possess many if not all the characteristics of a typical business it is quite appropriate to make use of a mechanism which can operate as an MIS "board of directors." The purpose of this group is the same as that of any such group, that is, to provide guidance and direction, and where appropriate, to approve policies and procedures which will strengthen the MIS business.

The analogy of the MIS function to that of a small (in some organizations a not so small) business within the larger organization is appropriate. Just as specific controls, reporting considerations, and direction are required to enable any business to realize its goals, so is it the case with MIS. In order to better appreciate the importance of the assistance which can be provided to MIS by this board of directors (the MIS steering committee), a review of the functions and responsibilities of the typical MIS department will help bring into focus the similarities between MIS and the typical business organization.

Some of the more obvious functions which are common to business in general and also to MIS are, Manufacturing, Accounting, Production Control, Sales and Marketing, Public Relations, and Long-Range Planning. Consideration of each of these functions will provide improved understanding, not only of the overall MIS function, but also of the necessity of adequate direction and guidance to that function. This is necessary to be certain that the MIS "business" is being appropriately managed, and as importantly, to assure proper correlation between MIS and the other departments of the organization.

CHAPTER IX

A detailed examination of the similarities between the various functions of the MIS department and those of a business will help clarify the issues involved. Perhaps the most appropriate place to begin is with the data center function.

The data center function of the MIS department is really a manufacturing operation. The data center is analogous to a factory in that it receives raw material (data) from any of several sources. This raw material may come into the data center as "batch" input; that is, input which is gathered in some particular location and when a certain quantity has been accumulated, it is sent to the data center. The input may be "on-line," that is, the data is submitted directly to the computer via cathode ray tubes (CRTs).

Regardless of the method used to bring the data to the computer, once that raw material (data) has been received, it is then processed in a series of operations which are very similar to a normal manufacturing process. These operations, edits, additions, deletions, or changes to existing files, sorts, printouts, or displays on CRT screens can be compared to a manufacturing process from which raw material is turned into the finished product. In the case of MIS, the raw material (data) is the input, the finished product (information) is the output. While information is the goal, it is often more accurate to state that the MIS output is in reality, processed data. The fact that many MIS installations often fail to produce true information as their finished product does not alter the data center factory analogy.

As is the case with any manufacturing process, the eventual production of a finished product is the ultimate goal. However, in the case of the data center production analogy, as is becoming the case in all manufacturing operations, "getting the product out the door," is not the only consideration. The quality of the completed product is an aspect of any manufacturing process which is beginning to gain increased attention! The quality of the data center product (information) should be of no less concern within MIS, than the quality of any output of a manufacturing process, be it automobiles, clocks, washing machines, or whatever. This concept of improved quality control is beginning to gain increased attention within progressive MIS departments.

The rise of quality control sections within MIS departments demonstrates the increased awareness of the importance of improved information quality. The concern with quality, as the management of the MIS function improves, will begin to assume a larger role in the MIS department. The emphasis will shift from simply completing processing runs on time, or bringing up a new system, to not only accomplishing these obvious goals (an often unrealized task in many MIS departments today), but to also strive for a continuing high standard of quality in all areas of the MIS function.

This awareness of and movement to improved quality is not by any means universal. Many organizations are simply too encumbered with poorly managed MIS functions to give serious consideration to improved quality, yet the general situation must change in time. As pressure mounts within organizations to become more effective competitively to at least maintain, if not reduce costs, and to provide improved service to the organization's customers, quality in all areas will become an increasingly important issue.

To carry both the manufacturing analogy and the concomitant question of quantity one step farther, the issue of data center scrap should be considered. An important factor in any manufacturing cost is the additional expense encountered because of scrapage. Even though in many factory processes the scraped material can be reworked, the cost can still be considerable. Of course, in the case of the data center operation, any scrapage (caused through computer reruns) is, with regard to the computer time, operation time, and printed output, completely lost. None of this work can be reprocessed; it is simply gone forever.

Clearly, anything which adds to the cost of a product or service diminishes the competitive position of the organization. When expenses rise, the competition enjoys an excellent opportunity to capture more of the market, provided of course they are able to better control their costs.

The issue of data center scrap costs are often overlooked or ignored in the consideration of overall costs of an organization's product or service. The actual product or service produced is irrelevant; it may be a manufactured item, insurance production, banking services, a hospital, or whatever. Little attention is paid to this question of additional expense caused by data center scrap due to two reasons, often those outside the data center, or perhaps the MIS department, do not understand how extensive and expensive this scrap can be, and often those in the MIS department do not relate this additional expense to increased product or service cost.

However, when items such as computer time, operators salaries, overtime, and wasted forms are totaled, the expense can be large. As an example, consider the case of a processing update operation which is carried on on the second and third shifts. Assume this production process requires eight hours of computer processing to complete. For whatever reason, it is discovered that the work processed last night must be done over, and in order to become current, twelve hours of overtime must be scheduled on the weekend. These costs are real. This situation is by no means an unusual occurrence in many data centers.

To these actual costs the intangible costs of missed deadlines, customer frustration and dissatisfaction, and the probable negative cash flow implication must be added in order to compute the real cost to the organization.

It is interesting to note the large number of data center operations which do not track the incident of reruns. Not only should this information be produced on a regular basis, it should be investigated and strong effort should be devoted to taking steps which will correct any serious problems. This is not to imply that a zero deficit plan should be attempted; errors will occur, inordinate efforts to halt all or most errors usually fail because people become too cautious and production suffers. A data center rerun goal, perhaps three percent of the total workload, should be set as an acceptable standard. As long as the total remains below that average, management should be satisfied.

The quality control function, as it applies to the effort of the data center, includes more than the correctness of the information produced. Attention must also be paid to the consistent, on time delivery of that information. This is a task which in many data centers, because of a lack of strong, effective management, often poses a difficult problem. One aspect of the problem is involved with the laoding and scheduling of the data center factory line (the data processing hardware) so that the work will be processed in the most efficient manner with regard to efficient management of that hardware, yet also guarantee that the work will be produced correctly and on time. This is, at its most basic level, simply a problem of successful and consistent adherence to the factory (data center) production schedule.

The issue of whether or not the data center hardware is being effectively utilized is one which does not receive appropriate attention in many MIS departments. While it is correct that the rapid declines in the cost of data processing hardware has made the issue of hardware expense somewhat less critical than in the past, the total hardware expense in most MIS departments is still sufficiently high to require management attention. The goal here should be to strike a balance, to provide sufficient equipment to handle the present and anticipated data center workload over a given period of time, yet to avoid insofar as practical, the installation of excess processing power.

While this may appear to be, and many MIS managers will claim it is, a very difficult task, it can, with proper management control, be achieved. Too many organizations today face one of two situations, either they have excessive processing power, which causes unnecessary expense; or, they have insufficient equipment, which creates service levels below those which are required to operate in a satisfactory manner.

Many MIS managers will claim, with some pride, that they have had the same equipment for a considerable period of time, perhaps three or more years and have therefore efficiently matched the data center hardware to the workload. Given the growth of the data processing demand in most organizations, if nothing has changed in three years, it can usually be argued that too much equipment had been originally installed. The factory analogy also applies here, this is an excellent example of factory capacity management.

Software, reasonably priced, is currently available which can be very effectively used to provide the information necessary to accurately portray current hardware utilization, and which can, with appropriate data, provide the basis for the development of very accurate usage forecasts. This exercise will require someone to analyze the information and to track the actual growth against the forecast. The cost of this endeavor can be more than offset by the benefits produced.

The current state of hardware technology is moving so rapidly that the price/performance curves are showing dramatic reductions. The competent MIS manager will stay abreast of these rapid changes and will work to take advantage of them. This is accomplished by knowing what his future short term (18–24 months) requirements will be, and then matching appropriate hardware to those needs.

In order to accumulate the required data which will provide the ability to forecast future growth, the data center must be aware of the anticipated changes in the workload over the time span covered by the forecasting period. To accomplish this, it is recommended as a part of each new project, or extensive change to an existing system, that an "impact statement" be prepared which will outline the anticipated hardware resource requirements. With this information, the total future resource requirement, over the life of the identified application or operating systems additions or changes can be quite accurately forecast.

This issue is important. It is not at all unknown to find situations where members of senior management are informed that, if they want this particular project to become operational, they must provide increased hardware resources. Often this bad news is presented rather late in the project development cycle, too late to drop the project without a large cost, so, senior management, having no choice, is forced to approve unbudgeted expense. Is this the result of MIS blackmail, or incompetency? Who knows? It makes little practical difference; in terms of the options open to senior management, the result is the same.

Adequate MIS controls, particularly in operational systems, are another important aspect of the MIS operation and one which the MIS steering committee must be aware of. The data center must be so structured as

OPERATIONAL IMPACT STATEMENT
For Project Number _____

Part I: Development   Date initiated _____
Section A: Project scope   Date revised _____
    1. Implement new system   Yes   No
       a. Number of programs   _____
       b. Number of jobs   _____
    2. Modify existing system   Yes   No
       a. Number of new
           programs   _____
       b. Programs to change   _____
       c. Programs to replace   _____

Section B: Development/installation schedule

	Activity	Begin date	End date
	1. Program testing	_____	_____
	2. System testing	_____	_____
	3. Acceptance testing	_____	_____
	4. Production release	_____	_____

Section C: Testing considerations
    1. Processing requirements
       a. Batch program testing   Yes   No
       b. CICS program testing   Yes   No
       c. Data Base Management System   Yes   No
       d. S/34 program testing   Yes   No
       e. CICS, S/34 communications   Yes   No
       f. CMS testing   Yes   No
    2. Processing facilities
       a. Disk storage   Yes   No
       b. Tape   Yes   No
       c. Printer and/or forms   Yes   No
       d. CRT or printer   Yes   No
       e. S/34   Yes   No
       f. Other   Yes   No
    3. Personal
       a. Data control   Yes   No
       b. Data entry   Yes   No
       c. Technical development   Yes   No
       d. Technical support   Yes   No
       e. Other   Yes   No
    4. Comments: If Yes to #2 or #3, please specify.

_____
_____
_____
_____

OPERATIONAL IMPACT STATEMENT *(continued)*

Part II: Production Environment Profile
Section A: Operational considerations

	Upon -----** Demand	Daily	Frequency** ----- Weekly	Monthly	Annual
1. Batch mode processing					
a. Number of jobs	_____	_____	_____	_____	_____
b. Partition hours	_____	_____	_____	_____	_____
c. Scheduling					
• Prime shift	_____	_____	_____	_____	_____
• Evening shift	_____	_____	_____	_____	_____
d. Printing					
• Number of reports	_____	_____	_____	_____	_____
• Total pgs/lns each pge.	__/__	__/__	__/__	__/__	__/__
• Total fiche pgs/lines	__/__	__/__	__/__	__/__	__/__
2. RJE/Batch					
a. Number of jobs	_____	_____	_____	_____	_____
b. Connect time	_____	_____	_____	_____	_____
3. On-line/Communications monitor					
a. Number transactions	_____	_____	_____	_____	_____
b. Other: _____	_____	_____	_____	_____	_____
4. Interactive/CMS					
a. Users/sessions	_____	_____	_____	_____	_____
b. Connect time (H.d)	_____	_____	_____	_____	_____

Section B: Resource requirements

	Number of Files	Est. Bytes Storage	File Type	Retention Days	CICS Access
1. Data sets					
a. Disk					
• Permanent	_____	_____	_____	XXXX	YN
• Temporary	_____	_____	_____	_____	XXXX
b. Tape	_____	XXXX	XXXX	_____	XXXX
2. Special forms	_____	_____	_____	_____	_____
3. Hardware	YN: Specify additional/replacement equipment.				

_____
_____

to provide the required control through all operational processes. This has to be accomplished so that anyone who relies upon the work being released can be assured that that work is complete and accurate. Too often, sound MIS controls are not built into systems when they are designed or, they are not given appropriate attention within the data center.

It is the responsibility of MIS management to see to it that, as standard procedure, adequate controls are built into all MIS systems, and that once in place, they are consistently used.

There are any number of examples of the unfortunate occurrences which can arise when proper system controls are missing or ignored. These problems range from minor inconveniences and perhaps embarrassment for MIS management, to horrendous disasters. The work carried on in the data center is of such critical importance to the organization, that work is so pervasive, that problems encountered in the data center reach far into other areas of the organization, often to its customers and ultimately to senior management.

It should be kept in mind when considering the question of data center controls, that with regard to the work in the data center, because of the speed of processing, what might constitute simple errors in many departments, errors such as the entry of an incorrect date, can become truly significant errors in the data center. Therefore, when problems do arise, they must be handled in the most effective manner possible. Adequate controls, coupled with strong data center management, can mitigate the effect of even serious data center errors.

The key here is not to carry out purges which will stamp out all errors forever. We are all human, errors do occur. The idea must be to build sufficient controls into all systems so that errors are detected as early in the process as possible and, once detected, that appropriate procedures are in place to correct the errors with minimum disruption. A serious flaw in many MIS departments is the failure to design systems geared toward "fail safe" conditions. In many instances much of the identification of error conditions can be done using the computing hardware. When errors are found, the system should be designed to make corrections, or to stop the processing as automatically as possible.

What are some of the consequences which may arise as a result of poor quality control within MIS? Many of these unfortunate results may seem obvious, yet mention of a few will help demonstrate some of the problems which can arise and perhaps more importantly, some of the ramifications to the organization. Problems such as, the issuance of incorrect customer invoices, shipment of the wrong goods to customers, incorrect calculation and billing of insurance premiums, failure to properly allocate and pay insurance claims, incorrect payroll calculations, posting of incorrect accounts to bank statements, or the failure to adequately maintain stockholder records, are only a few examples of problems which have occurred and which are traceable to improper controls.

These errors, and even more serious errors, will continue to occur. It is not possible to completely halt all MIS errors and it is not practical to attempt to do so. The emphasis must be not so much on the exclusion of all errors, regardless of cause, but to provide the means to identify those errors at the earliest possible point in the processing cycle. The goal should be to contain and correct all errors within the confines of the data center.

There is a linkage between sound, effective MIS controls and the issue of data center scrapage. Good controls will not eliminate all data center reruns, but good controls and strong management can reduce these reruns and therefore expensive scrapage, to levels which will be quite acceptable.

The issue of system design, of course, transcends that of effective system controls. Systems design, if it is to be effective and serve the best interests of the organization, cannot be carried on in a vacuum within the MIS department. The pervasive nature of these projects, their high costs, and the usually lengthy process required to bring projects to fruition, mandates sound effective coordination between MIS and the rest of the organization. This is simply necessary to assure that when these projects are completed, they do indeed support the goals of the organization.

The selection of nontechnical MIS projects and their overall management must be carried on as a cooperative effort between MIS and the client departments. This is an area where the steering committee can provide effective support.

The most effective approach, from the standpoint of systems which will best serve the clients, is to insist that the clients take the initiative in the selection and management of the organizations nontechnical projects. In the beginning, this may require the combined efforts of MIS management and the members of the steering committee in order to make progress. However, the concept that the nontechnical systems belong to the particular clients (not to MIS), and therefore are the responsibility of those clients (not MIS) is too important to be ignored.

The research and development aspect of MIS is just as important to the continuing success of the overall organization as is any other research and development effort in other parts of the organization. This is particularly true in view of the rapid rate of change within the data processing industry. Because of the accelerating rate of change of data processing technology, it is imperative that a continuing awareness of those changes and of both their potential benefits and pitfalls be recognized within MIS. Unless reasonable time, effort, and where appropriate, expense is devoted to MIS research and development the service level of the MIS function will decline. There are numerous instances of such situations today. The sorry fact is that in many organizations, while the effects of a "penny wise" approach may be apparent, the cause is not realized, or at least not admitted.

The concept of "pay now or pay later" is very much in effect here. Sooner or later, if the organization is to remain a viable entity, the changes in data processing technology must be addressed. There are options, a continuing attempt can be made to stay current with the technology, or it can be done in "catch up" stages, but it will have to be done. The most practical, least traumatic, and overall least expensive approach is to move to a position near the state of the art, and then remain there.

The question of developing a strong public relations orientation within MIS should not be overlooked. The typical MIS department suffers as a result of its usual dismal public relations effort. The work carried on within the MIS department is complex and difficult; many times the results actually produced are greater than the clients may realize. The fact that the clients may not be aware of the quality of the work is often due to a failure, not only to adequately tell the MIS story, but also due to a failure to treat the MIS clients as clients.

In fact, in some organizations, a negative sales effort is in place. Too often the MIS department is viewed as uninterested in the concerns of the rest of the organization or as adopting a cavalier attitude toward the rest of the organization. This is, of course, unfortunate! The complex, highly technical nature of the work carried on in MIS cause the clients of MIS enough concern; a failure to carry on an effective public relations effort which can mitigate at least some of the more pressing MIS concerns only makes matters worse.

Often in the press of day to day operations, the issue of effective, aggressive long-range MIS planning which will help improve the organization is not given appropriate attention. This is often the case because of the prevalent crisis management environment found in many MIS departments. The result is that, in many organizations, MIS is viewed (often with considerable justification) as being reactive rather than active. Because of the heavy reliance of the entire organization upon the MIS effort, this shortsighted approach will produce a deleterious effect on the entire organization.

The preceding will help demonstrate the similarities between the functions of the MIS department and those of any business. Given those similarities, it only makes sense to put in place a system which can effectively be used to provide both guidance and an objectiveness to the operation of the MIS department. Without such assistance, the chaos extant in many organizations regarding their MIS functions will not only continue, but in all likelihood will increase. The MIS steering committee is the mechanism which can be used to provide the required structure for effective guidance.

If it is to be effective, the mission of the MIS steering committee must be well-thought-out. Some of the more important considerations are:

- What is the scope of the steering committee effort?
- How should the group function?
- Who should make up the membership?
- What is the extent of the control to be exercised by the steering committee?

Careful consideration of these questions prior to implementation of the steering committee will help make the mission and performance of the steering committee much more effective.

The development of the steering committee should begin with the writing of the charter for the group (see example on pages 143-145). This document must address the function of the group in terms of its mission to provide guidance and support to both the MIS department and the MIS clients. This support should have as its goal, not only an attempt to link MIS to the goals of the organization, but also to provide improved communication between MIS and its clients. It should also be made clear through the MIS charter that the day to day operational concerns of MIS, and the management of the MIS department rest with the MIS manager, not with the MIS steering committee.

This is an important consideration; one which must not be forgotten as time goes on. The more aggressive members of the steering committee may, as they become more familiar with the workings of MIS, and the capabilities of its people, attempt to have certain members of MIS assigned to their projects. They may also attempt to control the scheduling of the data center work in order to suit their interests. It must be made clear, as a part of the charter, and when required the chairman of the steering committee must continue to make it clear, that the day to day operation of the MIS department is the purview of the MIS manager.

The goal in developing the structure of the MIS steering committee should be to have the membership represent the highest management level of the organization. The more senior the management group, the more effective will be its effort. Ideally, the steering committee should be composed of members of the senior executive group. While this is ideal, it usually will be difficult, perhaps impossible, to obtain a commitment to the steering committee from this level of management.

The success ratio for many MIS steering committees has not been particularly good. It has been estimated that the average life of a steering committee is eight months. One of the primary causes for such a poor record is the lack of support for the effort from senior management. Unless the steering committee is made up of senior level members, or unless it is very clear that senior management fully supports the concept of the steering committee, there is little chance of long term success.

There are sufficient examples of successful MIS steering committees. Those organizations which have been successful in this endeavor are those which have enjoyed clear senior management support. Unless the members of the steering committee realize that part of the judgment of their overall performance rests with the contribution they make to the MIS steering committee and with the success of the committee, they will not devote sufficient attention to the task.

One ancillary benefit of a steering committee composed of the highest level of the organization's management is that it provides an excellent opportunity for executives at that level to become more familiar with the workings of the MIS department, and of the opportunities inherent in the use of the technology. This increased knowledge of the workings of the MIS function can, over time, help senior management break through the aura of mystic which surrounds the MIS department. If this can be accomplished, a much more objective assessment of the value of MIS and the current MIS management to the organization can be made. In this respect, the effort required to actively participate in the MIS steering committee can pay large dividends.

There are several caveats which apply to the organization and structure of the MIS steering committee. The members of the committee must be organizational peers. An unbalanced steering committee, that is one which is made up of several members of the senior executive group and several department managers, will naturally gravitate over time to the control of the higher ranking members. This may occur in a subtle fashion, but it will occur.

In addition, it must be assured that all functional areas of the organization are represented within the MIS steering committee. The perception throughout the organization with regard to the steering committee must be that all areas are equally represented and that each area is given appropriate consideration in terms of the allocation of MIS resources. This is true even for areas which may not currently use any MIS services. Given the rapid strides being made in moving data processing into new areas of all organizations, it will only be a matter of time until these sections find a requirement for MIS services, therefore they should be represented from the beginning.

Once the organizational level at which the steering committee is to be made up has been determined, the next consideration is with the selection of the individual members. If the steering committee is not made up of members who are at the senior executive level, they should be appointed by a member of the senior management group to represent their functional area. This will help instill a realization of the importance of the appointment.

The success and effectiveness of the group is contingent upon the selection of people who will take an active interest in the steering committee and who will put forth the required effort to make the steering committee process successful. It will be much more effective and much more productive, if those assigned to the MIS steering committee have an interest in the assignment and also wish to increase their personal knowledge of MIS. Those selected should have a desire to improve the level of MIS service to the organization and be willing to work and learn in order to make a strong contribution. Those chosen should also be aware that participation in the group can help them learn more about not only MIS, but the other departments and functions of the organization.

The MIS steering committee should be formally structured and organized. A chairman must be appointed who will carry the responsibility for the effective functioning of the committee. While the manager of the MIS department should be an active member of the steering committee, it is not recommended that this person be appointed chairman of the group. The purpose of the MIS steering committee is to assist the MIS department; selection of the MIS manager as chairman of the committee will cause credibility problems. If the MIS manager becomes the group's leader, the feeling that the committee is a captive of MIS may arise.

It is entirely possible that an attempt will be made to install the MIS manager as chairman of the group. The stated reason may be that, because of the technical issues, the MIS manager, being more aware of those issues, is the ideal candidate for chairman. This is a spurious argument and it should be seen for what it is, an attempt to pass the responsibility to MIS. If the MIS manager must accept the chairmanship in order to move the group ahead, he probably should; but it will be much more effective if some other member of the steering committee is selected as chairman.

Of course, the exact authority and responsibility of the MIS steering committee will vary from organization to organization. If the senior staff and the Chief Executive Offices (CEO) make up the MIS steering committee, then it would seem reasonable to assume that the decisions reached by the steering committee would be binding. In those organizations not fortunate enough to have top level management on the steering committee, there must be a realization of the political aspects of the situation. That is, that any decisions made within the MIS steering committee are always subject to being changed or overruled by those at the highest level of the organization.

It is simply a matter of reality; at some time a decision made by the steering committee, although sound and clearly in the best interest of the organization, may be overruled at a higher organizational level. When this occurs, the members of the steering committee must be mature enough to understand this can happen and to accept the fact if it does happen and move on to other things. These situations are simply facts of business life and must be accepted as such.

A primary mission of the MIS steering committee must be to identify and pursue those MIS-related projects and issues which will best help the entire organization move toward its goals. The steering committee effort must be structured so that it is linked with the strategy of the organization as defined by the organization's leadership. The group must also deal with and, to the best of its ability, resolve issues of MIS policy and priority. In order to be effective, the MIS steering committee must be so structured and situated within the organization that all issues of any magnitude which touch upon MIS will come to the steering committee for resolution.

The MIS manager must be willing to make a commitment to both the concept and the realities of the MIS steering committee. If the clients find they are able to circumvent the steering committee by working directly with the MIS manager, or other members of MIS, if they find they can accomplish their goals without using the mechanism of the steering committee, the effectiveness of the group will be reduced. The members of the steering committee must make it clear to the members of their functional area that MIS concerns, other than day to day operational problems, are to be channeled through the MIS steering committee.

In order to make this approach effective, the management of the MIS department must appreciate the purpose of the MIS steering committee and must be supportive of the concept. Some MIS managers may view the MIS steering committee as a usurpation of their authority; however, the benefits to be realized from an effective MIS steering committee will outweigh any loss of control or authority suffered by the MIS manager.

As the MIS manager works with the MIS steering committee, it will become clear that the effective use of the steering committee is more a benefit than a determent to the MIS manager and the MIS department. As the burden of selection and priority assignment of projects shift from the MIS manager to the steering committee members, the job of the MIS manager will become less onerous. In this environment, the MIS manager will be able to devote more time to the management of the MIS department, to the development of the people within the department, and to the absolutely essential area of long-range planning.

What will have occurred will be that the typical MIS "balancing act" of attempting to be the sole arbitrator between all clients for the division of scarce MIS resources, will now shift to the steering committee. Most MIS managers would admit such a circumstance would be helpful for both MIS and the organization.

An important aspect of the MIS steering committee is the opportunity to provide improved communication between MIS and its clients at all organizational levels. Each member of the committee should accept responsibility for making certain the issues considered and the actions taken by the steering committee are communicated to those in the functional areas represented by that committee member. This communication flow will work to help improve credibility problems often associated with MIS. The fact that the news, good or bad, is coming from someone outside the MIS department will increase credibility.

Once organized, the steering committee should turn its attention to the development, or if they are already in place, the approval of a set of MIS policies. The MIS steering committee should ensure that a set of MIS policies are published, and that all who may be affected are aware of these policies. In many organizations the subject of such policies is viewed as something less than urgent. This should not be the case. While the development of such policies may indeed be a mundane task, the growing, rapidly changing nature of MIS mandates an appropriate level of control. Strong, effective MIS policies, which are updated when appropriate and which are adhered to, will help provide the required control.

The primary function of the MIS steering committee is to be found in the selection and priority of those projects which are to be computerized. A review of the manner in which this responsibility should be carried out will provide insight into the effort. The key here is to select projects which will have the best payback for the organization. A caution may be appropriate here. The payback may not always be in dollars; other, more subtle considerations, such as the effect on customers or competition, must also be considered.

A salient consideration should be kept in mind; it is quite possible a tendency to engage in "horse trading" may arise among members of the MIS steering committee. What may happen is that members will agree to support a particular project now for consideration of their project at a later date. This type of activity must not be allowed. The purpose of the MIS steering committee is to take an unbiased look at each project and to consider each strictly on its own merits.

There is also the very real danger that some members of the steering committee, through the application of superior selling skills, or force of personality, may be able to dominate the group, in an attempt to direct a disproportionate share of the MIS resource toward his particular interests.

This is likely to occur with members of the sales/marketing groups. Because selling is a normal function of their work, they will be able to mount effective campaigns to gain their objectives. It is not uncommon for members of this group to minimize the costs of the particular project and to adopt a stance which will claim immediate harmful results to the entire organization in the field if their requests are not accommodated. Such dire circumstances may indeed be factual, or they may not, in any event this is, if it occurs, an issue which the MIS steering committee members must address. This is one example of the requirement for a strong MIS steering committee chairman.

While it is not recommended that the MIS manager chair the MIS steering committee, that should not be taken to imply that the MIS manager should accept a passive role. Not only should the MIS manager act as an advisor on technical issues, in addition he must also bring to the board those technical projects and concerns which are, in his view, of importance. These projects should be presented as any other project and must vie for consideration along with other projects.

Some subjects which are technical in nature, and which should be fought for by the MIS manager are: Advanced or more powerful operating systems, system conversion projects, telecommunications projects, and data base projects. The potential of benefits such as these to the organization cannot be ignored. These could be examples of projects which will not provide an immediate payback, may even add expense, yet are critical for the future growth of the organization.

In order to make an informed judgment about the relative value of each project, a consistent method of presenting projects to the MIS steering committee must be developed and followed. A standard set of criteria must be developed which can provide a basis by which to judge the relative merits of all projects presented for consideration. The project evaluation sheet has proved an effective tool for defining potential projects.

In the consideration of projects for placement in the development schedule, project size should be considered. The total MIS manpower resource available during the project development being considered should be identified, and then projects should be scaled against that manpower resource. It is preferred to have a mix of project sizes in order to balance out the work and to avoid, if possible, the calamities inherent in attempting to bring two large projects operational at the same time.

Project size should be identified in terms of manhours, small (500–1000 manhours), intermediate (1000–3000 manhours), and large (3000–6000 manhours). It is not recommended that any single project exceed 6000 manhours. Any project over 6000 manhours, should if at all possible, be broken down into several separate projects. The reason for this is that

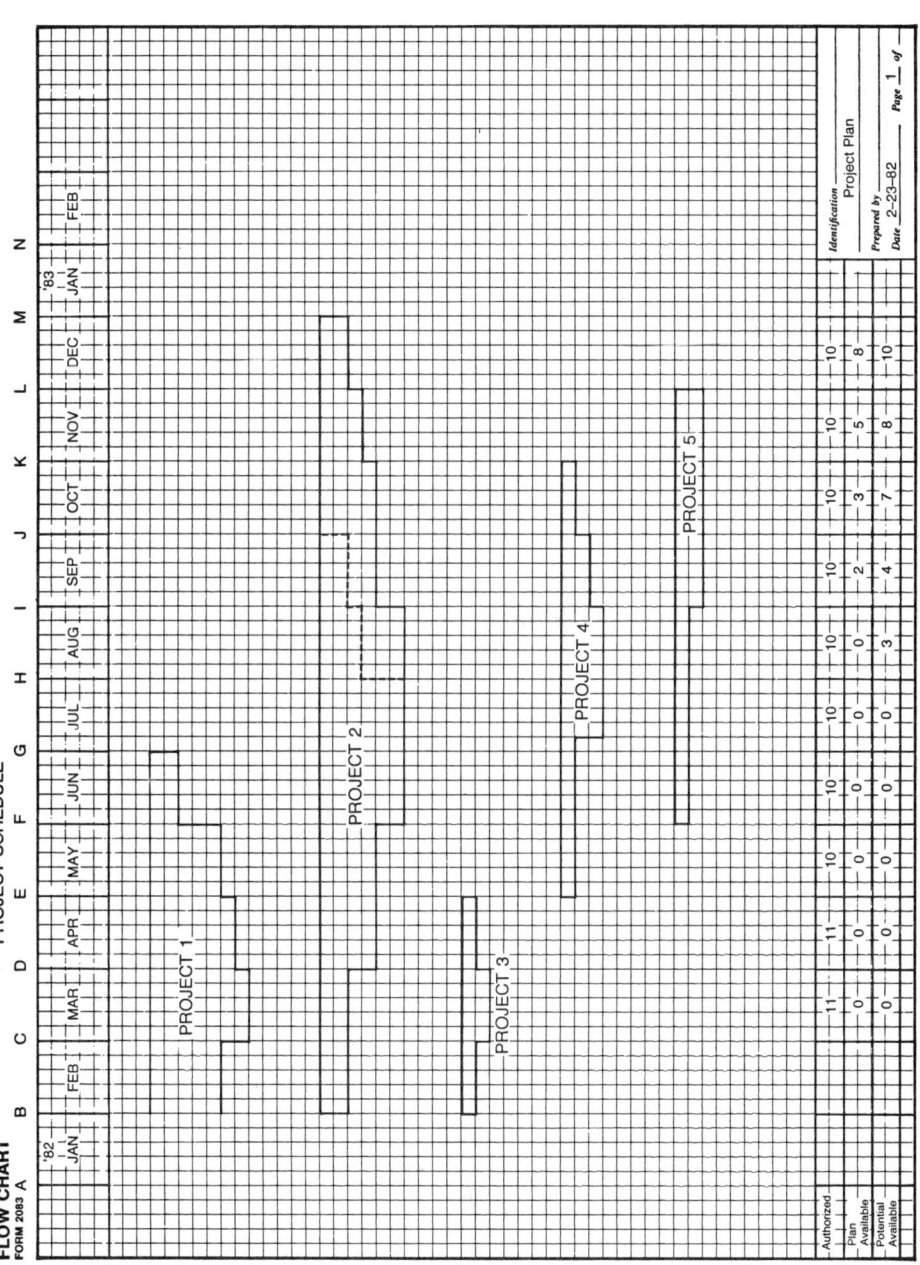

in most cases, projects over 6000 manhours are too large to be handled effectively as a single project. MIS must be involved in the determination of project size.

The presentation to the steering committee of requests for "immediate" projects should be held to a minimum and where possible, discouraged. Only situations such as clear competitive factors, regulatory changes or sudden changes in the organization's finances, should be viewed as reasons to consider (never mind approve) requests for immediate projects. Unless the steering committee adopts a firm stance, it will find itself reviewing a constant stream of "immediate" requests. The project selection process instituted by the MIS steering committee should be effective enough to inspire a planning disciple on the part of the MIS clients.

This is an important consideration. A real problem in some organizations with MIS performance revolves around a decided lack of control with regard to MIS project management. It is not unusual to find situations where partially completed projects are delayed, or even abandoned, because of pressure to direct resources to some new "immediate" effort. This is not only expensive, it is very frustrating, not only with MIS but for those clients who have had their projects adversely impacted. In those organizations where such situations occur, the MIS steering committee can provide an extremely valuable service to the entire organization.

The most appropriate approach to an effective project selection mechanism is to hold an annual MIS steering committee planning session. This should be a formal process, using the project evaluation sheets as the basis for the planning effort. Each member of the MIS steering committee should have solicited project suggestions from the appropriate members of their functional area. These projects should be detailed on the project evaluation sheets and those which have the most merit, the highest scores, should then be submitted for the assessment of the full MIS steering committee.

The information contained on the project evaluation sheet should be as factual and realistic as possible. The idea is to provide a basis by which all projects can be judged in order to select the overall best projects from the standpoint of the entire organization, not as a device to obtain a high priority and beat the other departments for scarce MIS resources.

The MIS project review session should be structured so that all members have equal time to present their projects to the rest of the group. The MIS manager must also be included in this presentation process. The idea here is that MIS technical projects should vie for scarce resources just as any other project. This part of the review will allow each member of the steering committee the opportunity to demonstrate the desirability of his or her projects.

After each member has had an opportunity to present their projects, the MIS steering committee should split into various groups to consider all projects and to rank the projects within their particular group. Once the rankings have been accomplished, the committee should meet as a whole to review the various rankings and to determine final placings. If a good job has been done, it is likely when the group reviews the placings there will be a great deal of similarity in the placings of each group. This consensus can be taken as an indication that those projects which have been given a high rating are indeed the most important from an overall organization standpoint.

Once the projects have been given their final priorities, a project schedule should be developed. The project workload should be spread out over the available time and resources. Within the scheduling process it is a good idea to attempt to intermix projects by size in order to maximize the use of the resources. Usually projects have more limited manpower requirements at the beginning and the end than in the middle, the idea is to avoid having too many people assigned at any one time to be effective or to find there are two few people available when required. This approach will require some shifting of projects within the overall project framework, but it is worth the effort.

Consideration of the development of the manhours per project is important. Much of the MIS credibility problem which arises in many organizations is due to a too optimistic estimate of project progress. Often, in the development of the total manhour estimate, as an example, a working day of eight hours is used as the estimation base. As a practical matter, the realistic figure, when breaks, meetings, illness, interruptions, and vacations are taken into consideration, is close to five or five and one-half hours per day. If the lower figure is used to estimate the length of the project in manmonths there is a greater likelihood of meeting the deadline.

The idea here is to arrive at a realistic figure and then to use that figure in all projects, regardless of size. As experience is gained, it will become increasingly easy to schedule projects which will, by and large, be brought in according to the plan. One of the real problems with MIS project scheduling is not so much in the determination of the scope of the project, but in the manpower allocation methods used to build the estimates.

Each project should also carry a built-in contingency factor in order to assure that the inevitable problems which will always arise, can be accommodated without endangering the total project schedule. A contingency factor, perhaps 15–20 percent should be standard in all MIS projects. Not to include a contingency factor, to assume that all will go well with no unforeseen occurrences, is simply naive.

PROJECT EVALUATION SHEET
Project Planning Review

Project description:	Functional area:
	Responsibility: (Requestor)
Is project now in work?	
Business objectives: (How does proposed project serve/support the business objectives?	
Benefits:	
Is project interrelated to other systems? ( ) yes Which?:	

PROJECT ANALYSIS

	Est'd man/months req'd		Project merit rating
	Systems	Users	(1 = low, 10 = high)
Estimated project costs ($000's)			
Functional specifications	$		Improved decisions
Systems design			Better control

Programming	Cost reduction
Test & debugging	Operations improv'mt.
Implementation	Regulatory requir'mts.
Training & indoctrination	Top mgmt. requir'mts.
Software	Timely information
	TOT.
Hardware	Total fig. of merit
	Urgency X 2 ( )
	Systems support by:
	( ) Functional area
	( ) MIS dept.
Other:	( ) Other, specify:
Total project costs:	Total project merit rating:
Estimated monthly continued (on-going) costs: $	Comments re costs:

Estimated timing (as proposed)

	1981				1982				1983	
	JAS	OND	JFM	AMJ	JAS	OND	JFM	AMJ	JAS	OND	JFM	AMJ
Specs												
Systems design												
Programming												
Test & debug												
Implementation												

Please continue necessary narrative on the back.

The problem with MIS project overruns is often due to unrealistic completion dates imposed by clients. The MIS steering committee must guard against this, and a formalized planning process is one method which can be used to help provide control. It is not at all unusual for the MIS manager to receive a decree from some department that project "X" must be installed by a certain date. The reason may be quite valid, but the completion date may be quite unrealistic. What then occurs is substantial discontent when the deadline is missed. An imposition of increased discipline on the clients with regard to MIS project planning and scheduling will help everyone.

The completed and approved MIS steering committee project schedule should be the basis for reporting progress against the plan until the next planning session is held and a new schedule is developed. It is also a good idea to review, for an appropriate priority, all projects on the schedule which have not been actually begun by the next planning session. The idea here is to make certain that all remaining projects which were approved are still valid. If this is not done, that is if these projects simply move ahead in priority, it is very likely other more urgent projects, unknown a year ago when this plan was developed, will not receive an appropriate priority. This applies only to those projects on which no work has begun. Projects which have been started should continue. While the planning session should be held yearly, the schedule should cover a larger time frame, perhaps thirty months. By doing this, everyone has a better idea of what is currently considered of value to the organization over an extended period.

The work of the MIS steering committee should include a provision for a postimplementation audit of at least selected projects. Some of the questions which should be considered are, implementation to schedule, quality of the system (particularly system controls), degree of client satisfaction with the system, and an assessment of the actual value of the project compared to the original claims for the project. This function might be best carried out by the organization's internal audit section; the purpose being to identify both the good and bad aspects of MIS projects and to use this information to provide improved projects in the future.

The use of the MIS steering committee is a very practical method to provide Board of Directors assistance to the MIS business. The benefits which can be derived from the approach offset any additional effort required to make it function.

One of the ancillary benefits of the group is that everyone, all members, gain from the experience. The non MIS members of the group will be forced to learn more about the MIS function and the functions of other sections of the business outside of their departments interests. The MIS manager not only gains required support for his effort, but he also gains an improved perspective, not only of the rest of the business, but also how the MIS function should operate in the organization.

The MIS steering committee provides an excellent vehicle for the improved awareness and education of those in other departments and in the executive levels of the organization about MIS. The MIS manager, through his interaction with the members of the MIS steering committee and through special presentations which he should arrange from time to time for the group, can make very effective progress in the effort to increase that level of knowledge.

As is the case with many MIS concerns, size of the organization should not be viewed as a constraint to the establishment of an MIS steering committee. Even in small organizations, the concerns and the issues will be basically the same; the implementation of the MIS steering committee can help any organization's MIS department become more productive.

Just as it is true with any business, the MIS business needs help in the allocation of its scarce resources. There is a decided tendency in many organizations to find that while the MIS department is going one way, the rest of the organization is headed somewhere else. The installation of a strong, interested, effective MIS steering committee can help make certain both groups move in the same direction.

CHARTER: MIS STEERING COMMITTEE

Purpose: To provide direction for profitable and effective computer-based systems within the organization. To further control the use of "computers" (as opposed to systems) so as to make certain the use of this equipment is both made known to senior management, and that its use is in the organization's best interest. To identify the organization's information requirements and to provide the appropriate planning, orientation, and review which will encourage the use of the MIS resource to help drive the business.

Scope:

1. Identify and prioritize the key management information needs of the organization.
2. Review and recommend to the Executive Committee a long-range plan for development of computer-based systems to meet identified needs.
3. Report to the Executive Committee on a periodic basis the current status of planning and results achieved since the last presentation.
4. Coordinate systems objectives and plans to effectively use the MIS resource.

5. Develop and implement specific evaluation and decision making procedures for planning, monitoring, and prioritizing systems in terms of resources, time, business strategy, and profitability.
6. Review all systems proposals for approval/disapproval and ranking in accordance with established system development plans.
7. Review/monitor project status compared to approved proposals for corrective action.
8. Become, and remain, aware of major developments in information technology in order that systems plans and objectives reflect the latest advances in cost-effective techniques.
9. Monitor the deployment of Systems and Programming resources between maintenance, data base, and new project requirements.
10. It must be understood that the responsibility of the MIS Steering Committee does not extend to the day to day operational concerns of MIS. The day to day management functions of the MIS department are the purview of the MIS management.

Generalizations for the Steering Committee

1. The approval of projects (any effort over eighty manhours) and the assignment of priorities for those projects rests with the Steering Committee. The MIS department will participate in addressing the technical feasibility of projects and will work with appropriate users to prepare the proposal information for presentation to the Steering Committee. Requests for Immediate Programming (less than eighty manhours) must be approved and prioritized by the appropriate Steering Committee member.
2. We currently deal with projects in three size categories:

   - Small—from 80 to 500 manhours
   - Intermediate—500 to 3000 manhours
   - Large—in excess of 3000 manhours

   Experience demonstrates that we should not engage in more than one large project at any given time. Whenever practical, projects of intermediate and large sizes will be broken into phases. This will provide the following:

   - The MIS department and the user will be better able to accurately judge project progress, a milestone approach can be used.
   - Users will be able to work with some of the output and therefore determine its value prior to completion of the entire project.
   - We can test the appropriateness of the project as it moves ahead. This will help avoid the situation where redesign and programming become immediately necessary at the end of the project, because circumstances have changed.

3. We have changed some of our design methods. We are now using a process we have designated "Standard Project Management" (SPM). This has been set up to provide improved discipline within the staff, and better control projects. We insist that the bulk of the planning, and a reasonable amount of the documentation, be completed prior to the start of programming. Without an approach such as this, the tendency is to begin programming too early, really before sufficient information is available and thus a lot of work ends up being redone. The concept of a separate documentation group is also new to the corporation. We are insisting that the required documentation be produced on a phased basis throughout the project cycle. This helps assure that, when the project has been completed, the documentation will also be complete. The user documentation is the primary responsibility of the user. MIS will assist in this effort, but the user must carry most of the effort for his area.
4. The "Systems" really belong to, and are the primary responsibility of, the client departments. MIS provides the technical skills, advice with regard to the feasibility of the proposed system, and will participate in the proposal preparation. However, the client, in particular the client project manager, must understand and accept the ultimate responsibility for the system.
5. We need to understand that approval of systems and technical approaches made at a given time can have a long-range heavy impact on MIS. The cumulative effect of even a series of small projects will, as they become operational, force us to increased equipment expense. This is not to imply that this is a bad thing, but only to make you aware that today's excess capacity has a way of disappearing very rapidly.

CHAPTER X
The Concept of Data as a Valuable Organizational Resource

The concept of an organization's data having significant value, of it in fact being an organizational asset, has begun to gain acceptance within a number of organizations. The idea, and the perception of the value and importance of an organization's data will gain increased prominence as more data processing work moves to an "on-line" status. The more that data is disbursed throughout the organization, and as more people come to rely upon it and to require it on an immediate basis, the more "data" becomes in fact "Information," the greater will be the realization of the value of that data as an organizational asset. As this occurs, it will become increasingly obvious that the incompleteness or loss of this data will pose a serious threat to the organization.

The realization of the value of the data to the organization is somewhat analogous to the growing awareness of the absolute requirement to protect an organization's computerized data from loss or destruction. Although this realization is by no means universal, a general acceptance of the requirement to protect the organization's data, to secure it as one would secure any other assets of the organization, has begun to emerge in the more enlightened organizations. During the years when the data processing function consisted of punched card processing, little, almost no, attention was devoted to the issue of protection of the data (cards) so that work could be carried on in the event of a disaster. Unfortunately, much of this disregard for adequate security of the data is still with us.

It has only been in the past several years, in particular with the advent of the passage of the 1977 Corrupt Fair Practice Act, that serious attention has been focused on the issue from a senior management level, and therefore caused increased concern within MIS departments. This growing awareness of the requirement to protect the organization's data is also an indication of the growing awareness of the value of data.

There is simply no question that data is a critical component in the ongoing function of the organization. As the amount of work processed by computers grows, the requirement for clear, accurate, well-protected, and readily reproducible data becomes more obvious. The parallel awareness to protect that data, based upon the unfortunate experiences of organizations which have had their data destroyed, is also coming to be recognized as a business necessity. It must become clear to anyone who gives the matter some thought, that the organizations which will become and remain successful in the future will be those which are able to capture, control, understand, and then effectively use their data. This consideration of an organization's data is not restricted to the particular organization's internally generated data, but also to data about the industry, service, customers, and competition which the particular organization deems important.

Those issues addressed in the preceding chapters of this book, specifically the distinction between data and information, the delivery of information in the most economical and rapid fashion to those who have need for the information, the continuing declining costs associated with computing hardware, improvements (often dramatic) in data processing technology, improved awareness within MIS departments of the requirement to use sound management techniques, and most importantly, the increasing understanding on the part of the organization's senior management of the real value of data and more appropriately information, make the effective recognition and use of data within the organization a paramount issue.

The desire, the need, for sound information within all organizations cannot be denied. It must be clearly understood, however, that that information cannot be provided without the underlying data. Further, the information can be no better than the quality of the underlying data. In some cases, and the concern may grow as the use of computers grow, a lack of data may be of more benefit, in the long run, than the use of faulty data which will encourage the organization to make incorrect decisions.

While the importance of data to an organization cannot be denied, there is still a great deal of work to be done in many organizations to make the awareness of this issue more widespread and to begin to develop and install a plan which will assure that the data, once identified, is managed in an appropriate manner. This plan, as is the case with a number of other MIS issues, must be begun by the organization's MIS department. As is the case with other MIS issues, forces outside MIS, probably at the senior management level, will be required to make things happen. Consideration of the question of the value of an organization's data will help put the issues in better perspective. Once the issues are better understood, progress can begin to improve the situation.

Concept of Data as a Valuable Organizational Resource 149

While much currently needs to be done in the typical MIS department to gain effective management control of the existing data, forces outside the department are creating new situations which will only exacerbate the problem. The rush to the use of small "stand alone" (independent) data processing hardware, while often very effective and easily cost justified, has in many instances overlooked several very important organizational issues. This is not meant to imply that there is anything wrong with the use of such equipment; its use, where cost justified and where a more effective alternative is not available, represents a sound, logical way to produce results. In these circumstances, the use of such equipment should not be restricted.

However, the area so often ignored with the stand alone processor explosion is that of control of the data. This is really not too difficult to understand when the circumstances are carefully considered. Because the issue of control and protection of the data has, in all likelihood, not been raised by the MIS department (where reside the "data experts"), it is simply not realistic to assume that neophyte stand alone computer users will understand, never mind be concerned with, the issues.

This is a subject which, after more than twenty years of growth in data processing, is only now beginning to receive appropriate attention in the data processing industry. It is ironic that apparently much of the trauma, frustration, and unnecessary expense associated with the growth of data processing will be experienced again as the use of stand alone processors grow. This subject may well be the greatest cause of information processing difficulty for organizations in the future.

The same scenario which has led to a great deal of the difficulty with MIS, difficulty which still exists, can be seen developing in the arena of the small processor. The vendors are targeting their selling efforts toward unsophisticated, first-time users. As was the case with the early, and to some degree current, marketing of large scale systems, questions of control, operation, backup security, and documentation are obscured by heavy selling of the potential benefits. Because these areas are often not given appropriate attention in the organization's MIS department, they do not appear to be of concern to those considering installation of their own small processors.

What has any of this to do with the question of the organization's data? It has taken traditional data processing departments a long time to recognize the difficulties and unnecessary expense associated with inaccurate and redundant data. In many organizations the growth of data, often redundant data, has gone on apace. As the volume of computing work grows and as more of that work is carried on outside the normal confines of the MIS department, the issue of control and effective use of all organizational data becomes increasingly critical.

The availability and growing use of Data Base Management Systems (DBMS) has provided tools which can help address the issue of improved data and of the reduction of redundant data. The growing use of Data Base Management Systems has begun to address questions about immediate access to data, of using that data to produce information, and to begin to reduce expense and confusion through the reduction of redundant data.

However, the use of the DBMS is not, of itself, a panacea. Unless appropriate structure and control of the tool is provided, the problem of redundant data and the production of data as opposed to information, will only grow. This fact coupled with an uncontrolled ability on the part of those outside MIS to create their own data poses problems which must be addressed.

Consideration of the question of data will show that there are two main classifications of data within an organization. The recognition of these distinct data types and the development of approaches to classify and control each type are pertinent to the issue of consideration of an organization's data. While they are admittedly somewhat ambiguous terms, the identification of data as "organization" and "departmental" will help segment the two basic types of data.

For the purpose of this discussion, the distinction is as follows:

- Organizational data can be described as that data which has specific use in more than one department of the organization. Examples would include, general ledger, claims, inventory, or payroll information.
- Departmental data would be that data which has a very narrow use, limited at most, to one department and perhaps to only one person in a department. Examples might be, tool crib parts, salesmens' routings, or budgets.

The identification of the several types of data within the organization is important. It should be clear that the care, custody, and control of organizational data falls within the purview of the MIS department, and it must be understood to be a part of that department's responsibility. That data classified as departmental, that is, data which does not carry organization-wide significance and which is restricted to a specific department of the organization, is the responsibility of the particular department which generates that data.

This is an important distinction. As the automation of data continues to grow, and as much of this growth occurs outside the traditional MIS department, it must be clear to everyone who has responsibility not only for the various data but also the programs and supporting documentation required to process that data into information. It is not practical, and it is certainly not appropriate, to assume that because it is all data MIS has the ultimate responsibility.

Concept of Data as a Valuable Organizational Resource 151

The idea of the responsibility for departmental data residing within the individual department is not something new. This is no different than the particular department manager being responsible for the papers filed in the department's filing cabinets. In fact, much of the work transferred to computerization, either through use of mainframe processors, personal computers, or word processors is work which has been stored in file cabinets in the department in the past. It is important that the distinction of this departmental data be recognized, and that the organization's MIS management be relieved of the responsibility for data (even though "computerized") over which it does not maintain any control.

If, for whatever reason, agreement cannot be reached to define the different types of data within the organization, and to whom the responsibility for that data falls, it is very likely that at some future date, trouble will arise. As an example, MIS has the facilities, and should have an operational procedure to backup its data files so as to be able to provide copies of the data in the event the original files are lost or destroyed. However, if it is not clear who owns certain data or whether or not the data should be backed up, what happens if the data is destroyed? Should that data have been considered of significant importance to be either adequately protected within the particular department or placed under the control of MIS?

It is clear that potential disasters await some of those department managers who have arbitrarily gone their own way often without the knowledge of their supervisors, with regard to the use of personal computers. What may occur, subsequent to one of these disasters, is a rush to a strengthening of controls, of the installation of safeguards which should have been installed in the first place. Perhaps a large number of nonMIS people will find out what many MIS people have learned the hard way, once data is totally gone, it is gone forever.

Concern with the security of data is not being accorded appropriate emphasis in many organizations. Usually the organization's payroll data, for obvious reasons, is secured, often through very elaborate procedures, yet very little is done to safeguard other data. The primary onus for failure to pay appropriate attention to data security must fall upon MIS management. Members of the MIS department must become much more aware of the absolute requirement to both control and protect that significant organizational asset: data. Unfortunately, it often takes a near disaster, or publicity about a real disaster in some other organization, to produce an awareness of the problem at the senior management level of the organization which will prompt MIS to take action.

The question of security of the data is a multifaceted one. All aspects of the question must be considered; some will, after a review, not appear too worthy of any action and can be forgotten; others, of course, will require much more attention. The concerns are the same, whether the data under consideration happens to be organizational or departmental. Some of the more salient aspects are, loss of the data through occurrences such as accidental cause, employee error, or malicious destruction, vandalism, fire, flood, or building collapse. In some organizations the issue will also extend to questions about the protection of certain confidential data from competition.

As an example customer lists, product pricing policies, or new product proposals may be of great interest to competitors. How this data is protected from the competition can be a very serious issue. Unfortunately, many people in the lower levels of MIS, who have control over much of this data, are not made sufficiently aware of its value to those outside the organization.

As more of the organization's data resides in some type of electronic form, and as increased computerization assures this will occur, the more vulnerable the organization becomes. As an example, the old concern with the honesty of the organization's cashier or accountant, has extended to those who have access to the computer room, or to the files used on the personal computers. There are two issues here. One, that of altering the data in order to produce fraudulent invoices, insurance policies, or checks is a problem which must be considered and dealt with. A second less obvious, yet if sufficient backup steps are not in place, more critical situation is that of malicious destruction or removal of an organization's data.

This is in fact a situation where one person, without a need for assistance from anyone, can, if conditions are right, bring even the largest organization to disaster. Destroying files which have not been backed up, such as payroll, accounts receivable, cash transactions, policy registers, or savings accounts records just to name a few, can in fact signal the end of the organization. Or, it may be rather than destroy these files, the employee simply chooses to use the files to extract ransom from the organization. These situations do not represent some abstract speculation, such occurrences have arisen in the past, in all likelihood they will occur again.

The preceding should make it clear that the vulnerability of the organization's data, and the potentially severe consequences associated with that vulnerability, must be fully appreciated. That appreciation cannot be limited to the MIS staff, management in other departments of the organization and the appropriate members of senior management must also become aware of that vulnerability. It must also be remembered that consideration of the protection of the organization's data cannot be done retroactively; once destroyed, if not properly backed up and protected, the data and more importantly, its value to the organization, is lost.

Concept of Data as a Valuable Organizational Resource 153

The subject of data redundancy is one which many organizations must address. The fact is that many organizations already have too much data, simply because much of that data is redundant. This fact has begun to become apparent as Data Base Management Systems (DBMS) begin to enjoy greater use in organizations. The analysis of the existing data resources required to install a DBMS and to begin the design required to use the system effectively, very rapidly points out the existence of this data redundancy. One of the positive aspects of the use of the DBMS is the ability to reduce, often by significant amounts, the data required to carry out the various MIS functions.

If data is an important organizational asset, why is the existence of redundant data undesirable? The costs associated with the storage and manipulation of excess data can be considerable. The control of that data, in terms of being certain that the correct files are being used in processing runs in the data center, can be an enormous task when a number of similar files are in constant use. The task of identification of those files which carry certain data and those programs which access those files, in a nondata base, data dictionary environment can also be enormous. This situation represents unnecessary expense, unnecessary effort, and increases the risk for the occurrence of errors. It would be difficult, probably impossible, to determine the cost to any particular organization associated with the burden of redundant data. Several examples can help illustrate both the scope of the problem and its magnitude.

Consider an organization, in reality a typical organization, which over the years has developed a series of systems which involve information about its customers. This information might include items such as, purchases, shipping information, customer mailing lists, salesmens' call routings, accounts receivable, to include some, but by no means, all the uses of the customer data within this particular organization. For each of these individual systems, assume that a separate customer master file has been developed and is actively used for that particular system. Of course, it can be argued, that although the information contained in each customer master file is essentially the same and that with appropriate care and control in the original design of each system at least several of the separate customer master files would not have been needed. That, however, was not the case.

These types of situations are not uncommon. The author is aware of one installation which, at one time, had thirteen separate, active customer master files, each used for a different customer information system function. What that meant, of course, was that any change of customer information, addition or deletion of customers, change of address, change of name, and so forth, meant subsequent changes to twelve other customer master files. Any time a system using customer information was to be processed, it took careful control within the data center to make certain the correct master file was being used and that it was the latest version of the customer information. This was no small task for employees of the data center.

In this case, the introduction of the Data Base Management System and the use of a Data Dictionary process provided the opportunity to reduce the information contained on the thirteen customer master files to one comprehensive file which could then be used in all customer information systems. The result, in addition to the obvious saving in data center time and confusion, was less tape usage and storage and a positive method for control and security of the customer information through the use of the data dictionary.

While the preceding is a rather straightforward example of the savings in time and effort, and the increase in control and security which can be achieved with the use of a Data Base Management system, many more dramatic examples can be found. It is, of course, correct that the DBMS will require increased hardware resource compared to nondata base processing. However, this increased usage can be mitigated to some extent through the use of effective system design under the DBMS. As has been stated elsewhere in this book, data processing hardware has become dramatically less expensive in the past several years; progressive organizations will take advantage of this fact to vastly improve their MIS functions.

The perfunctory installation of a DBMS is not a panacea; care must be taken when embarking on the DBMS effort. There are a number of systems available, and as is the case elsewhere in the data processing industry, some are very good, some are not. Because of the high cost associated with the purchase, installation, and ongoing support of the DBMS, care must be exercised in the selection of the package; this will be a long-term commitment; it must be as correct as possible.

The high quality Data Base Management Systems available are not all alike; some have particular strengths in one or two areas, some in other areas. Each organization, through its MIS department, must determine what it wants from its DBMS, and then select a high quality system which best fits their needs. There is probably no ideal data base system for a particular organization, but having devoted the time to think the issue through in order to have a clear understanding of what the organization hopes to gain, and what it is willing to pay, will make the ultimate selection less difficult.

There are several subtle traps in this question of the selection of a DBMS which need to be considered. First, because this is a "big ticket" item, and its selection has implications outside the package itself, MIS should expect considerable vendor pressure to be applied in order to influence the selection. Again, the more carefully the requirements of the package and the goals desired for its installation have been thought through, the better prepared will MIS be to withstand and answer the contentions of the various vendors.

Secondly, as the work goes on to address the issue of selection and installation of a DBMS, it will become apparent that, while there are a number of options available, any of them will require a significant amount of time, effort, expense, and risk. Often, as they get into the investigation process, members of MIS management become fearful of the magnitude of the effort. Reasons, often apparently reasonable reasons, are advanced to delay the investigation of the DBMS. This simply should not be allowed. The installation will not be any less a task several years in the future; the best approach is to make the most informed decision possible and get on with the job.

Of course, reduction of data is not the only feature of the DBMS. The ability of the MIS clients to gain access to data in a much more straightforward manner, without the interaction of MIS, and to then be able to manipulate that data through their own effort, to change the data into the information they want, when they want it, may be the salient factor in the consideration of the DBMS.

The Data Base Management System should provide the use of "high level" programming language. This is a programming language which can be easily understood by nontechnical people who can then use the language to develop much of their own information.

However, many MIS installations are reluctant to provide this access to clients because of fear of losing control of the data, and subsequently some of their power, or because of the increased processing power required to support this environment. This cannot be allowed. Unless the DBMS once installed is exploited to its fullest, much of its potential will be lost.

This is why the DBMS plan must be in place prior to the selection of the package. A clear understanding of what is required, what will be offered, and how it will help the organization move ahead prior to selection, will make the success of the DBMS much greater. Once the requirements for the DBMS have been identified and those involved with the selection agree that those requirements are both correct and reasonable, consideration should be given to the method which will be used to move the organization to a DBMS environment.

A number of different approaches can be considered. Too much emphasis on looking at all the possible approaches and their variables will tend to obscure the real issues and delay progress. Often situations such as this become devices to avoid making decisions. It is better to develop several practical scenarios, select the one which is most appropriate for the particular organization, and then get on with the job. The key is to make use of the DBMS as rapidly as possible, once it is installed.

Consideration of three basic approaches should suffice. The options should be to either attempt to move, as rapidly as possible, the existing systems to the DBMS, without attention to a redesign other than that necessary to accommodate the DBMS (and, of course, to redesign all new systems for the most effective DBMS processing), or to select a date after which all new development will be placed under the DBMS, and all existing systems will be converted as they are rewritten over time. The third approach is to institute an effort to rewrite all existing systems to operate in the most effective manner under the DBMS. While the particular plan used is an individual decision, it should be realized the third option is the most massive and, if selected, should be done with full knowledge of the time and effort involved.

The concern should be that a plan is decided upon, senior management support is obtained, and that the effort begin. The development of the plan, the support of the organization's senior management, and a commitment on the part of both parties to the project will overcome the false starts, processing disasters, failures of the DBMS effort, and in some instances, the eventual abandonment of the Data Base Management System installation which has occurred in some organizations. The imposition of appropriate investigation, planning, and control instead of an enchantment with the technology can assure success for the DBMS.

The installation of the Data Base Management system affords an excellent opportunity to make vast improvements in the control and availability of the organization's data. This can be accomplished through the development of the data administration position and the use of a data dictionary system. As is the case with the DBMS, specific steps to implement both of these functions depend upon the perceived needs of the particular organization; yet some general comments regarding both may provide some insight to the topic.

These issues, the installation of the data dictionary function and the establishment of the position of data administration, are bound to cause disruption and at least a degree of concern within both the MIS department and the client departments. These are really manifestations of some of the "cultural" problems alluded to earlier in this book, as is the case with other cultural problems, they must be dealt with as they arise. The introduction of the DBMS will generate some degree of trauma in any organization, the resistance to change is universal. As organizations enter into the DBMS world, power groups may begin to form within various sections of the organization, including the MIS department. These groups will exert pressure to gain control of, or to obstruct, various functions of the DBMS effort.

Part of this contention will be based upon the desire to either gain additional power, or to attempt to avoid the loss of existing power. It may also spring from a reaction to a fear of change, an attempt to maintain the "status quo." Often, more resistance and reaction will arise within the MIS department rather than the client areas, but a certain degree must be expected from either area.

Strong leadership is essential if a successful Data Base Management System is to be installed and effectively used. Unless those who make up the organization's MIS management have a clear vision of what they want from the DBMS, and unless they are willing to support that vision regardless of the effort required, success will prove to be very elusive. Consideration of some of the issues likely to develop with regard to the data dictionary and data administration will provide the opportunity to anticipate some of the probable areas of concern.

The data dictionary should be viewed as the "front gate" of the DBMS. The dictionary should be used to exercise stringent control over all data which will be placed in the DBMS. Not only the data itself, but also the pertinent documentation about that data, should also be put into the dictionary. If the choice of the data dictionary, which may or may not be an integral part of the DBMS, is a good one the issues of control of and information about the organization's data can be achieved. Whether or not the full potential of the data dictionary is realized then simply becomes a function of the willingness of MIS management to demand that the data dictionary be used to its fullest extent.

Resistance to the data dictionary can be expected within the MIS department. Members of the department will not want to prepare the documentation which will be a required part of the input for the data dictionary. If the process is appropriately structured, if the documentation rules are enforced, over time many of the documentation concerns prevalent in most MIS departments can be overcome. This will require a great deal of patience and determination on the part of MIS management, but it can be done.

As a practical matter, what can the installation of the data dictionary do for the MIS department, and much more importantly, for the entire organization? The data dictionary will assure the identity of the organization's data elements; it will also provide definitive information about which systems use those data elements. Assume as an example, a decision to move to the use of the expanded zip code number.

Without the availability of the Data Base Management System and the data dictionary, the task, if there is any volume of customer activity within the organization, can be massive. The first step in the process, obviously, is to identify those programs where zip code is used. This means any program in the system which might appear to use zip code would have to be examined. Once the programs are identified, no small task in many organizations considering the state of their MIS documentation, all such programs would have to be changed, recompiled, tested, and placed into production. This could indeed require several man years effort in a large, poorly managed, MIS department.

With the data dictionary and the DBMS, the task is considerably easier. The data dictionary would be accessed to provide, automatically, a list of all programs which use the data element "zip code." Then, the size of the zip code data element would be lengthened, the appropriate programs changed, tested, and placed in production. In addition, as an offset of the work being done, the task of changing the documentation to show the changed status of the data element, zip code, would also be accomplished.

A serious fault in most MIS departments over the years has been the existence of what might be best described as the "Shoemaker's Children" syndrome. Too often, the MIS department fails to use the power of the computer to improve the function and control of the work MIS is attempting to accomplish. If MIS management will find the fortitude, both within the MIS department and with senior management, to use these tools to help itself, real improvements in the MIS service level can be achieved.

Any number of data base management systems have been installed without the concomitant installation of a data dictionary. This is not entirely the fault of the MIS management; it has only been recently that effective data dictionary systems have been offered. The data dictionary has evolved, to some degree, because many installations attempting to operate a DBMS without some type of data dictionary have found, to their chagrin, that the DBMS by itself has not been enough. The DBMS may do the job it has been promised to do, but without the front end effect of the data dictionary, control is difficult, in some installations impossible, and as a consequence, much of the value of the DBMS is lost or at least diminished.

While the imposition of control and the demand for much improved documentation which will come with the data dictionary will cause dissention within MIS itself, the issue of the function and power of the data administrator will probably cause more disention over a much wider area of the organization. Prior to consideration of the data administrator function, the meaning of the term as it will be used here must be explained. The position of data base administrator would, for the purpose of this illustration, encompass the technical functions associated with the operation, and control of the data base management system and the data dictionary which would report to the data administrator.

The data administrator would be considered the czar of the organization's data. This person would, if necessary, act as the final arbitrator with regard to any issues concerning the organization's data. The political ramifications inherent in such a position can be immense. The concept of one person who carries ultimate responsibility for the coordination, direction, and, where necessary, enforcement of rules regarding the organization's data, both within the MIS department and throughout the entire organization, will raise any number of questions and concerns; yet it must happen if the DBMS is to be used to its full potential.

The generation and the excessive proliferation of data within most organizations will continue over the coming years. The control of that data must become a substantial issue in most organizations in the future. A number of subtle issues are involved in the consideration of this question, and they deserve to be examined in some detail. The effort to move toward the reduction, and where practical, the elimination of redundant data is one issue. The "ownership" and security of data—who can see, who can change, and for what purpose—is another question. The transfer of data from one client's files to another's files to allow more than one client to use the same data for different purposes is another issue. Who should have the ability to alter data on-line, in a real-time mode, and the ability to provide appropriate audit trails to determine who did what to, or with, the data must receive increased attention.

In addition, the ability of the MIS department to recover from the loss of the data base, to bring the operation back on stream, and to continue the processing as if nothing has happened, will also become an increasingly important issue. These are all issues which will fall within the purview of the data administrator. Another subtle issue has come into play here; loss of the computer will, of course, bring clients who depend upon the computer to a standstill; loss of the Data Base Management System will have exactly the same effect even though the computer itself is available.

The question of where, within the organization the data administrator should report, and at what level the position should be placed, are difficult issues. A strong argument can be made that, as the position develops, it should be placed outside MIS, perhaps at a higher level in the organization than that of the senior MIS position. First, however, the position must be instituted and developed. In order to begin the process, the data administration function should be located in the MIS department. This, of course, presumes an interest on the part of MIS management to move the function forward.

Prior to the installation of the data administration function and the selection of a particular person to fill that position, time should be devoted to consideration of the content of the position within the organization. Also, if time is provided to allow the data dictionary and DBMS software to be installed and to allow people to become comfortable with those processes, the job of selection of the data administrator will become less a gamble, simply because more will be understood about what the position entails within the organization. In addition, the development of the position will be less of a political problem, because the data dictionary and the DBMS, if correctly handled, will have built some credibility for these new approaches.

During this period, considerable time and thought must be given to accurately defining the duties, responsibility, and authority of the data administrator. Unless a clear case can be made otherwise, it is probably most appropriate to begin the function within the MIS department. The rationale for this is simple. MIS has the most technical experience, and hopefully (although in many cases not realistically) MIS management will possess the vision to work to make the function effective.

That data which is resident upon the data center hardware, and currently under the control of MIS can be rather easily managed. Appropriate software can be installed which will help assure that control. As the ability of the clients to do their own data processing work, either through the information center concept, or through the use of stand alone processors, increases and becomes more commonplace, the amounts of data within the organization will grow, in all likelihood, that growth will be dramatic. How is all this data to be controlled? By whom is it to be controlled? These are questions which must be addressed and resolved.

As an example, the question of "ownership" of the data, that is, who controls the data and decides what additions or changes can be made to that data and who else in the organization can have access to that data will become a significant issue. Some areas are, by their nature, straightforward and will not cause any particular problem. Payroll data clearly belongs to the payroll department and should be under its control. The general ledger data is the purview of the accounting department.

In those somewhat more ambiguous areas, the questions of description, ownership, and use of specific data elements will raise far more significant issues in many organizations. Because little attention has been paid to this issue in the past and because any attempt at control is almost nonexistent, the facts of both data redundancy and of the ambiguity of data elements has grown to the point where, in many organizations, it is out of control.

Part of the blame for this problem must lie with the organization's data processing departments. Much of the redundancy and ambiguity have arisen as a result of acquiescence on the part of the management group to foster the "creativity" of the members of systems and programming. The spurious contention has been advanced, and unfortunately often accepted, that programmers should be allowed to do whatever they wanted in terms of the definition of data elements; hence the problems currently found in many organizations.

While the fault does lie with poor programming and design practices, the introduction of the DBMS and the data dictionary allow the ability to exercise proper control. It is correct, in many organizations a large, perhaps an inordinate, amount of effort will be required to clear up the situation, but the tools do now exist. Whether or not MIS management will be able to find the fortitude to properly manage these issues remains to be seen in many organizations.

Some examples will help illustrate the problem. A data element which identifies a customer may be found to carry the following identification in various systems within the organization—Customer Number, Cust. No., C.N., or C0. N0. It must be kept in mind that each of these four designations mean exactly the same thing and that they all identify the same customer information, that is, customers of the organization.

A second example might be that of the use of part numbers in a manufacturing organization. A part numbering system may be in place which is used to identify the components of the products produced. The data element used to identify the item, "part number," may appear as follows in different systems, P.N., Part Number, P.Number, or Part Numb. Again, regardless of the different specific identification, the data element, part number is the same.

To add to the confusion (as if any more were needed), each functional area may have developed a unique part numbering scheme. As an example, part number 1786 may identify a particular component in one area of the organization, and it may be used to identify something entirely different in some other area. Or, it may identify a part of an assembly in one section, and a part of a totally different operation in some other section. Such occurrences are not unusual, particularly in organizations where no attempt has been made to integrate systems; where in effect, everyone has been allowed to go their own way.

While the preceding examples have a manufacturing bent, the implication must not be drawn that these problems are somehow isolated to manufacturing processes; they are universal; they fall across the entire MIS spectrum. The introduction of the data base management system and the data dictionary afford real opportunities, not only to provide improved accessibility to the data and to allow clients to better handle their own needs, they also provide the opportunity to clean up the organization's data.

In many organizations, because of a history of failure to install and enforce MIS standards, the building and maintaining of redundant data

162 CHAPTER X

elements has become a way of life. Clearly, one of the necessary functions of the data base administration effort will be to eliminate such inconsistent or redundant data. It is obvious, when the data element, "Customer Number" or "Part Number," are identified throughout all systems and have exactly the same meaning throughout the entire organization, a great deal of unnecessary effort and confusion can be eliminated.

The accomplishment of this process will not be easy, it will require time, patience, money, and a serious senior management commitment if it is to succeed. The person appointed to the position of data administrator must be a strong individual; someone who can withstand the political pressures which are certain to arise and to become issues as the process is put into place.

The data administration process not only will work if it is properly managed and supported; it can produce sound benefits to the entire organization. There are organizations where a very good job is being done, where the results are evident; there must be many more in the future if organizations are to grow and prosper. While the data administration effort, in many organizations will be massive, the technical consideration, if the effort is properly managed, will not be as critical to success as the political considerations. This fact must be recognized at the onset and plans must be made to handle the issue.

Any effort to address the issue of an organization's data must not ignore consideration of the question of the security of that data. The issue of security of the data should be broken into two segments, the actual security measures used to protect the data, and concern with those procedures and processes which will provide the ability to continue the operation of the organization in the event of the loss of the organization's computing power. Clearly, the data is of primary importance to the organization; yet if there is no ability to continue to capture, maintain, and process that data, the potential harm to the organization can be immense. Unfortunately, these twin concerns, that is, the protection of the data and the ability to continue processing in the event of a disaster (contingency planning) receive less than adequate attention in most MIS departments.

The first consideration must be protection of the data from loss through any of a number of occurrences. The most obvious threat is often seen as fire, yet there are any number of occurrences which can prove to be just as serious. Some of these are, flood, building collapse, earthquake, theft, or malicious acts either from outside the organization or by employees, equipment failure, or power malfunctions to name a few of the possibilities.

One example, which has occurred in the past with disasterous results, yet which can be controlled with very little cost, is where an employee has simply removed external computer tape labels, while at the same time destroying the manually maintained backup records. What this means is the organizations data is still extant, yet who knows what is what. This has been carried one step farther, where data files which should have been saved have been written over and the essential data has been destroyed. In this case the data is gone forever. These conditions can, of course, come about through accident as well as from malicious intent. They can be controlled through the use of a tape management system for a very nominal cost. Even so, many organizations do not have such systems installed.

This is really hard to understand, when such a system, which will absolutely protect the data, can be installed for something less than six-hundred dollars a month. When this cost is considered against the damage which can be incurred, there should be no reason for hesitation in installing such a system.

There have even been instances where employees have removed computer tapes which have contained valuable organization data from the data center and either held them for ransom, or have sold them to competitive organizations. While the installation of a tape management system cannot control theft of tapes from the data center, the point is that organization's data is much more vulnerable than is often recognized.

The data is also vulnerable from other sources of potential danger. As the use of on-line–real-time processing increases, the risk associated with the manipulation of data arises. There are several methods which can be employed to help protect the data from unwanted manipulation. These methods are available through the use of software which can be used to impose controls such as passwords and to secure files. In addition, sufficient MIS audit controls must be in place so as to be able to determine what has been done to the data, and where appropriate, who has had access to it.

The question of reconstructing the data and of the ability to carry on the organization's operation in the event of a disaster, regardless of the cause, simply cannot be disregarded, even though that is indeed the case in many organizations. It is not an exaggeration to state that the organization's data may indeed be the organization; it is certainly correct to state that loss of the data, or the occurrence of a circumstance which precludes processing of that data, can mean the demise of the organization.

The only way to provide for continued operation in the event of an MIS disaster is through the use of a well-planned, regularly updated MIS contingency plan. The Corrupt Fair Practices Act of 1977 places severe penalties on an organization's senior management for losses which can be traced to a failure to adequately protect the organization's data. The data processing manager can also be held liable for losses under the 1977 Corrupt Fair Practices Act. Therefore, it is incumbent on many members of an organization's management to protect the data and the ability to process that data.

Contingency planning can be accomplished in any of several ways. A total in-house approach can be used, where everything is done by the organization's own people; or, a contract can be initiated with a firm (there are a number of reputable firms) which will carry out the complete effort. Much has been written on the subject of contingency planning, it is beyond the scope of this chapter to provide detailed information on the subject. The purpose here is to raise the issue, to alert readers to the absolute requirement to move ahead with contingency planning.

The data is indeed a valuable organizational asset. Awareness of this fact becomes greater all the time; those organizations which have come to recognize this fact, and to move with appropriate dispatch to control, protect, and effectively use the data will be the winners in future.

CHAPTER XI
The Future

A number of issues have been emphasized throughout this book. Some of the major themes have dealt with issues such as commitment, both on the part of MIS management and the organization's senior management, the application of sound management practices to the MIS function, an aggressive use of state-of-the-art techniques, a willingness to accept a reasonable amount of risk in the development of progress for the MIS effort, yet a tempering of that risk so as to avoid a "bet the company" approach.

Failure to recognize the absolute importance of these factors and to take the required action to address them has been responsible for much of the universal MIS difficulty encountered today. Considering the current state of information processing technology, it is quite correct to state that, "given time, patience and a high-quality staff, anything requested of the MIS department can be produced." The key is the willingness to recognize this fact and then to take aggressive action to move the organization ahead.

The astute MIS manager will accept a role of catalyst in order to use the advances in the technology to push the organization ahead. This will not be easy; it can often be very frustrating; yet it is in everyone's best interest to make known the real potential in the technology.

There is ample evidence to support the fact that very positive results can be obtained by a well-managed MIS organization which enjoys both high-level support and interest. In those organizations where MIS has been recognized as being valuable and important, where a strong commitment to high-quality information processing has been made, much is being accomplished.

A fundamental requirement is the need to have MIS management which possesses the vision to perceive the real benefits which can be produced from a high quality, aggressive MIS effort, and who are willing to step up to the important issues and to fight for them. This is not an easy task, it can be frustrating, and often seems to be unrewarding for those most involved in the process. However, the potential return to the organization cannot only be substantial, it will in many instances, mean the continued success of the organization.

Of course, the first concern must be to stabilize the basic MIS function. Until this is accomplished, until the crisis mode can be done away with, very little real progress can be made. There must also be a reasonable degree of flexibility in order to be able to take advantage of the rapidly changing and improving information management techniques. When this environment has been developed, the stage is set for real information processing progress.

If one will devote sufficient thought to the subject, it will be seen that those organizations which are not willing to embrace the new technology, which continue to add people to solve their information processing problems, are headed for serious difficulty. Those installations where all systems are "handcrafted," "in-house," where programs are poorly written, where documentation is nonexistent, will over time find themselves in great difficulty.

Indeed, MIS departments in a number of organizations face that exact situation today. It may not yet be apparent, but the day of reckoning is at hand. Many executive committees face the prospect of being dismayed to learn that large sums of money are going to have to be spent, not to move to leading-edge technology, but simply to correct the accumulated problems of the past. This will come as a real shock, because in many of these organizations the MIS function will have been viewed as being well run. The absence of visible, severe problems does not necessarily mean all is well in MIS. This is particularly unfortunate because much of the cause of the problem can be traced to MIS management inertia.

This problem is likely to be exacerbated in the coming years. That which has occurred in the past ten years in areas of advances in information processing technologies is certain to appear to have been rather insignificant compared to those changes and advances which are likely to occur in the next five to ten years. So much is being done, in so many areas, that much of what was speculative even a few years ago, is now rapidly becoming the effective standard for information processing.

One obvious example of this growth of the technology can be seen in the area of *microprocessors.* Less than five years ago, the use of microprocessors was little more than a curiosity, limited in most instances, to very special areas. Today of course, the use of microprocessors is not only an accepted business fact, they are changing both the manner in which information processing hardware is used and many of the prior concepts about the development and uses of office automation.

In spite of this, there are a number of MIS managers who simply refuse to have anything to do with microprocessors, and who will make absolutely no effort to offer any alternatives. There is no doubt that such a stance is harmful to the organization, yet it is a rather common stance. This will change in time, but in many organizations the change will be very expensive, frustrating, and lengthy.

An important, probably a critical question, which must now be posed in all organizations is "will the next five years see our use of information (not data) drive the organization forward, or will that span of time see the organization fall behind the competition as a result of failure to fully appreciate the value of information, and to so position itself that it can consistently make the best use of the increasingly rapid change in information processing technology?" While this should be considered a critical question for all organizations, it will in all likelihood, based upon past experience, not receive appropriate attention in many organizations.

The uses of information processing technology are becoming increasingly ubiquitous. As that use continues to spread beyond the confines of the MIS department, as more people who possess neither technical skills or interest become exposed to the benefits inherent in the process, it is clear that the demand for improved information, produced on a more rapid basis, will continue to grow. Certainly, those organizations which are best equipped to accommodate these growing demands will find themselves best positioned to use the technology and to recognize the subsequent advantages offered by that technology.

There is sufficient proof available today to substantiate the contention that, properly managed, the use of the existing technology (both the hardware and software) to "leverage" the investment in that technology into very large returns is not only possible, but is a very practical method. Those organizations which have made an appropriate commitment and which have done a good job in this endeavor have seen dramatic results. While the best one can do is to speculate about the future, it seems safe to maintain that, given the probable advances in the technology, these dramatic results will continue.

There are examples where, through the use of the technology, a single application has been developed which has provided a tangible payback which is equal to, or larger than, the total investment in the advanced process. In such a situation, of course, all the other benefits achieved from the uses of the process can be considered a bonus. One example is that of the use of the information center concept in a manufacturing organization to provide timely information about scrapage in a production process. The total ongoing annual expense for the information center is approximately $2 million; one application (out of a current total of 115 applications) will generate an annual scrap saving of $½ million.

Conversely, there are a large number of organizations which will face monumental difficulties with the improvement of their MIS functions. Sooner or later it will become obvious that the organization, in most cases through inertia or fear on the part of the MIS management, has become locked into obsolete technology. The effort to remove themselves from such a situation will not only be costly, in many organizations in the millions of dollars range, but it will also greatly inhibit MIS growth.

MIS functions do not remain static; they either grow or they begin the process of deterioration. It is ironic that when MIS functions reach a particular plateau, often times, rather than continue to help the function grow, senior management takes the attitude that, because everything is being done well, support can be shifted to something else. This, of course, is foolish. Over time these MIS functions deteriorate, the process is usually subtle and it takes a while, usually at least several years, to become noticed. When the service level reaches a low point, senior management reacts, spends a great deal of money to bring the function up to a reasonable level, and then unfortunately, allows the process to begin again.

This, of course, comes back to the question of commitment to the MIS function. The effective MIS function is built upon long-range planning which, using the new technologies, implements the plan on a phased basis. Because of the long-range implications, the effort cannot be carried out on a "start, stop" basis and be successful. It is the duty of the MIS management to prepare and push the plan. Once accepted, senior management has a responsibility, not so much to MIS as to the entire organization, to provide the required funds to support the plan. If the commitment is not ongoing, the process of degeneration sets in, and any progress made is ultimately lost.

The correctness of the preceding assertion can be verified rather easily. A review of ten randomly selected organizations would show that over the last ten years at least seven will have gone through one or perhaps two "reorganizations," probably through the process of bringing in a new manager; and it is likely that at least several of those organizations will have had more than two MIS managers in that time period. This is most unfortunate, once an MIS function is operating well, it should be encouraged to grow and develop, not starved off.

Many organizations face at least several major problems with their current MIS functions. These are problems, which, in many instances are not even being considered. The problems center around questions such as, how is the current function, based upon obsolete technology, a function which in all likelihood is becoming increasingly unstable, to be managed? What approach is to be adopted to move the organization to a position where the benefits of the new technology can be realized; and, once there, how can the organization remain current with the changing technology?

While a number of manufacturing analogies have been used throughout this book to illustrate important points, one more is appropriate in order to make a final point. It should be noted, that while manufacturing situations have been the primary focus (because of the author's background), the principles which have been addressed apply to all types of organizations.

There is, in many manufacturing organizations, widespread use of the manufacturing data base system "DBOMP."* This system has been obsolete for perhaps the last five years. Often, because MIS management has felt personally comfortable with the use of this system, not only has little effort been expended to restrict its use, it has in fact been integrated into nonmanufacturing systems in many organizations.

Because DBOMP is an obsolete system, support from the vendor is minimal. In addition, there is, as is always the case with obsolete software, a declining number of people who understand the intricacies of the software. This means that a number of organizations are becoming increasingly vulnerable through the continued use of this software. In spite of this situation, the issue is being ignored in many organizations. One reason for this is because it is a technical problem. In many installations the current MIS management is comfortable with the DBOMP software and therefore sees no reason to change.

This situation cannot continue. It is only a matter of time, in many installations a very short time, before the issue of DBOMP will become a very serious problem. The cost and trauma associated with the removal of this obsolete technology will be considerable. To make matters worse, the example of DBOMP is only one of several, perhaps a large number, of other such issues. Senior management must mount and maintain an effort, in the absence of such an effort being undertaken within MIS, to make certain the organization is not being unduly exposed to such dangers.

The organization's senior management can be assisted in this effort through the use of outside consultants. The selection and use of a qualified MIS consultant can be of great help in moving the MIS department in the right direction. Of course, the introduction of a consultant into the MIS environment will usually cause disruption in the MIS department and will be resisted. The degree of resistance to the use of consultants will usually be found to be in direct proportion to the level of the quality

---

* "DBOMP" is an obsolete manufacturing Data Base Management System.

of the work being done in the MIS department. That is, the worse the quality of that work, the greater the resistance.

The quality of consultants, as is the case with anything else, varies. The selection of a good consultant with the requisite background and experience is critical. Talking to others who have used the services of the particular consultant can be helpful in the selection. The services of a good MIS consultant will not be inexpensive, but, if the advice given is followed, the results can be outstanding. One point should be noted in considering the selection of consultants. Sometimes the person who makes the initial presentation, often a very sharp, very capable individual, may not be a member of the team assigned to the consulting project. Whoever selects the consultant should make certain exactly who will do the work and the extent of their qualifications.

It is also the case, once the consulting assignment has been completed, that the advice rendered is ignored. Senior management must be certain that adequate follow up is carried on so that the recommended actions are carried out. It is interesting that an organization will spend a quite considerable sum to engage a consultant and, once the assignment has been completed, lack the fortitude to see that the required actions are taken.

The typical MIS manager carries too much technical baggage! Too few MIS managers are viewed (or appear to want to be viewed) as managers. The truth of this statement can be very easily verified by attending several MIS seminars. It will very quickly become apparent from both the general conversation and from the questions asked, that many of the people in high-level MIS management positions still have a very high technical orientation. "If this is the case," it might be asked, "why are there so many technical problems in MIS departments?"

The answer, at least in part, is that while many of these people do indeed have a technical orientation, that orientation is still focused on the technology they feel comfortable with, which is in many instances, obsolete technology. What is working here is the result of inertia, induced at least in part, through the process of the manager having become comfortable with his position. Where MIS is little understood, perhaps feared, until the function reaches a crisis stage, little will be done to move ahead if the management of MIS will not take the initiative.

This is going to change. Computer literacy is rapidly becoming a fact in the United States. Increasingly, people entering the work force are not only familiar and comfortable with the uses of computers, but they expect to be able to use the computer as a routine part of their job. It is not at all unusual to find certain disciplines, such as engineering graduates being interviewed for their first job, inquiring about the degree of computing power which will be available to them. If use of the computer is not an aspect of the job, many of these potential employees will not be interested. This will become an increasingly important aspect in the job market in the future.

Those organizations which have not taken appropriate steps to provide a reasonable array of information processing tools to their individual workers are certain to find themselves unable to either attract or retain high-quality people. While this is just beginning to appear as a problem, it is certain to become a widespread concern within the next five years. It is not only likely that not only will information processing facilities have to be made available, but also as the state-of-the-art advances, they will have to be made increasingly sophisticated if high-quality people are to be attracted and retained within the organization.

This will not only be true for those who work outside the MIS department, but for members of MIS as well. It is clear that as competition for those people who possess really high-level MIS skills increases, the sophistication of a particular organization's MIS function and the technical opportunities and challenges available will become an increasingly critical factor attracting these people.

Conversely, people who do not possess at least a basic knowledge of computers will find it increasingly difficult, not only to advance their own careers, but also to continue to find employment. Those who ignore these facts will suffer the consequences.

The issue of the use of data base technology and the concomitant availability of "fourth generation" programming languages is an excellent example of this expanding knowledge and use of information processing. This issue presents several areas of opportunity and concern. The traditional MIS department must become much more flexible in its approach to addressing MIS concerns. The concept of the "computer utility" is very close to becoming a reality, in fact it is just that in some forward looking organizations today. The data processing programmer will increasingly lose importance as more of the work is done outside the MIS department.

Those people currently employed in MIS departments who cannot accept the changes which are clearly coming, face difficult times. The issue of buying much of the required applications software in the future, rather than building everything in-house, will also present difficulties for those in MIS. Other areas of MIS, such as computer operations, data entry, and data central will also undergo change. Organizations must become aware of these developments and take the required steps to make these transitions as painless as possible.

The problem here is that, based upon the evidence, those currently managing MIS functions have not been able to provide leadership. Will they do so in the future? It is rather unlikely that they will do much on their own volition to either change the basic structure of their MIS functions, or to attempt to prepare the people in their departments for that which is certain to occur.

As has been stated elsewhere in this book, the responsibility for the growth and development of a sound, forceful, forward-looking MIS function is not the sole responsibility of the organization's MIS management; senior management must also be willing to accept a role.

While it may at first appear mundane, and not worthy of the attention of senior management, one example of the requirement for increased attention from senior management can be found in the issue of data versus information. Concern with the details of the subject are not a part of the purview of senior management, of course, but this group must, as their organization enters the data base era, pay more than the usual cursory attention to the subject, or suffer the consequences later on.

If sufficient involvement is not forthcoming, the uses of advanced technology are likely to exacerbate the issue in the future. This does not mean that members of the executive committee must become computer technicians, but that rather common circumstance, where members of the group tend to abdicate most of the planning and overall direction of the information processing effort to the MIS group, must change. As an example, there is no question that the issue of more effective organization, control, and use of the organization's data must occur in order that a true information processing environment be developed.

In order to accomplish this goal, there must be direction and support from the organization's senior management. If that direction and support is not made available, the work carried on in this area will have an MIS flavor. This may not, in the long run, be in the best interest of the organization. The MIS functions which will be the most productive are those whose work is closely linked to the strategy and goals of the organization. There must be a linkage between the organization's goals and the MIS direction which affords sufficient flexibility so that, as circumstances change, either within the organization, or with information processing technology, MIS can respond and continue its support without the requirement to redevelop the entire MIS world.

Because of the rapid growth and change of information processing technology and because of the impact of these changes upon the organization, it is imperative that a "change management" approach be brought to the issue of adapting the technology to the organization. The idea of charging management within the MIS department to control the impact of technical changes is rather widely used; it has definite benefits outside the MIS department.

The concept of change management is to identify the components of a changing situation, identify insofar as possible, those components which will likely cause problems, prioritize the components by relative importance, and work to manage the changing environment. The idea is to assign specific responsibility for various areas to people and to develop an action plan to attack the problems.

The benefit of a change management approach to use of the developing technology is to be able to, through the identification of real and potential problems, not only gain control of the rapidly changing environment, but to also be better able to determine how the various components of the technology can be effectively fitted together in order to use the technology to drive the organization ahead.

The change management concept, if used correctly, forces stronger communications between MIS and the rest of the organization. Regularly scheduled meetings between members of MIS and those in other areas of the organization who are being affected by the changing technology provide forums to not only solve current problems, but if handled correctly, to identify potential problem areas and to move to stabilize those areas before they get out of hand.

It will be incumbent upon organizations to recognize the dramatic and rapid information processing changes they will face in the coming years; and to begin now, to consider these issues and develop strong plans to use the technology in order to position the organization so that whatever is required to both accommodate and capitalize on those changes are in place and can be effectively used to address these issues.

The concern on the part of the members of an organization's executive committee that MIS "costs too much," must change. That is not to indicate a blanket statement that all money spent on MIS in every organization is spent appropriately or wisely, of course not! What must occur, is a realistic appraisal of what is being returned to the organization for the investment. Decisions must be made about, first, whether or not that return is sufficient, and then, about how much more can be realized from various spending level increases.

No one would think they could purchase a luxury sedan for the price of a compact car. The same holds true for the MIS function. All the results and benefits can be obtained only if the senior management group is willing to provide the required support and then see to it that the expected results are delivered.

It comes down, of course, to a series of choices. What is possible for a given level of spending? How will those results benefit the organization? What are the long-range implications of spending, or not spending, to a certain level on the MIS effort? The problem is often to be able to identify those choices and to be able to correctly determine what can be produced at various spending levels.

Those organizations which are fortunate enough to currently have strong well-run MIS functions are in a very good position to make these judgments, based upon current performance, and to, probably, be better able to justify increased support to continue the effort. Whether or not they will capitalize on this situation depends upon the organization, but if they do not they will lose real opportunities.

There is a real linkage between the growth, the continuing success, and the ultimate viability of an organization and the quality of its MIS function. However, as the technology race becomes faster and as the real value to be had from information processing becomes increasingly clear this fact will become much more apparent. Some organizations, unfortunately, will find this out too late for it to be of value to them; they will not be in a position to overcome what they have allowed to occur through years of apathy.

The payback, the real use of the technology, is not in the ability to place a CRT on the desk of each member of the executive committee and provide instant, perhaps rather unimportant information on the screen. It is to be found in managing the organization at the middle levels, in presenting options and accurate information on potential problems, on trends on possible opportunities, on accurate forecasting and modeling, on the reduction of costs in all areas, and in improved service to the organization's customers. Those organizations which do this well will be the winners in the decade of the 80's and beyond.

Fixed Asset Accounting— Statement of Requirements July 14, 1981

FIXED ASSET ACCOUNTING—SYSTEM REQUIREMENTS

Problem Definition

The fixed asset accounting system currently in use is inflexible, not comprehensive, and does not provide information that *is* maintained in a timely, useful manner for today's reporting needs. It provides minimal data on depreciation and current book values and only then at year end. Additional information is needed that could be readily provided to support specific retrievals, investment tax credit, accelerated depreciation range (ADR), and replacement cost reporting (FASB 33) on a more timely and cost-effective basis.

The current system was developed by the corporation in 1970. It has proved to be of limited capability and inflexible in the light of recent changes in governmental regulations, and increased demand for other fixed-asset information.

1. Timeliness of information is restricted to monthly input, edit and summary, quarterly updating and error reporting, and annual book value reporting. Errors are identified quarterly. Depreciation, fixed asset balances, and surplus equipment lists are available only at year-end.
2. The information maintained is not complete and comprehensive enough for today's needs. There are not enough asset classification codes or enough description space to identify the assets for all the processing required. Current replacement costs, acquisition costs, and other data are not readily available. Separate tax depreciation cost schedules and useful lives should be maintained by the system at the asset and specific asset group level.

We should also be able to identify an asset as real or personal, exempt or nonexempt for investment tax credit purposes.
3. The current system is not flexible or powerful enough to do the job necessary. Identification of reporting entities such as company, division, or location is difficult. There is no automatic interface with the general ledger system—maintenance and balancing must be done for two systems. Depreciation must be calculated manually for the year in which as asset is acquired or disposed of. Accurate depreciation and book value are available only at year-end. Planning projections of depreciation expense and asset balances in the future must also be done manually. Another function not currently supported is the production of transaction lists that categorize capitalizations, sales, dispositions, and so forth. Other system reports needed would support accelerated depreciation range reporting (ADR) and Financial Accounting Standards Board (FASB 33) reporting of asset replacement costs. Also, the current system will not allow the input, maintenance, and reporting of leased asset data.

Proposed Solution

The current fixed assets accounting system should be replaced with one that provides more complete, accessible, and timely information suitable for the corporation's current and future needs.

In replacing the fixed assets system, Corporate Accounting would remain the primary user and be responsible for data input and maintenance. In addition, the Tax Department, Business Project Planning and Analysis Department, and Facility Engineering would be concerned with system capabilities. Representatives from these areas will be participating in directing the project.

A construction in progress (CIP) system has been considered as an adjunct to this project. Preliminary study shows that most of the expressed needs for a CIP system can be relieved by capitalizing promptly and classifying completely when the item is put into use. Several procedural changes are being implemented or reviewed to improve the timeliness and consistency of input.

The solution will be successfully complete with the implementation of a new fixed asset accounting system that provides:

1. Input, complete editing, and reporting of transactions on a monthly or more frequent basis.
2. Functional reporting monthly or upon demand for:
    A. Current depreciation and book values (see Exhibit A).
    B. Projected depreciation and book value for a future time period (Exhibit B).
    C. Transaction history (Exhibit C).

Fixed Asset Accounting 177

EXHIBIT A
Current Depreciation and Book Value—Report Content

Report usage:

To provide accurate expenses and assets on financial statements—Income Statement, Balance Sheet, and Cash Flow.

Report content:

Fixed asset identification—company, division, location, department, account, and tag number (major and suffix)
Description and classification codes
Acquisition date and cost (book)
Depreciation
Depreciation reserve (book value)
Depreciation method

Totals by company and location for depreciation expense and depreciation reserve.

EXHIBIT B
Projected Depreciation and Book Values—Report Content

Report usage:

To provide accurate expenses and asset values according to current and forecasted data for use in preparing annual budgets and long-range plans.

Report content:

Fixed asset identification (company, division, and so forth)
Description
Depreciation method
Depreciation—projected for quarterly periods at least one year into the future

Totals by company and location for depreciation by time period.

3. Classification and data retrieval for:
   A. ADR reporting (Exhibit D).
   B. FASB 33 reporting (Exhibit E).
   C. Investment tax credit reporting (Exhibit F).
   D. Machinery and equipment surplus and location lists by category (Exhibit G).
   E. Real estate, personal property, and tax reporting.

178 FIXED ASSET ACCOUNTING

EXHIBIT C
Fixed Asset Transaction—Report Content

Report usage:

Two versions of this report would provide:
1. A cost summary of additions, retirements, adjustments, and so forth by fixed asset class.
2. A detailed audit trail showing activity for each fixed asset.

Report content (financial summary):

Fixed asset identification
Beginning balance
Additions
Retirements
Transfers
Adjustments
Ending balance

Totals by company and location for all dollar values.

EXHIBIT D
Federal and State Depreciation Reporting

Report use:

To identify tax depreciation by class for federal and state income tax returns.

Report content:

Asset guideline class
Fixed asset identification
Tax information
    Asset life
    Depreciation method
    Acquisition cost
    Depreciation cost
Retirement gains and losses

Totals by company and location for cost, depreciation, gains, and losses.

EXHIBIT E
Detail for FASB 33 Disclosure

Report usage:

To meet requirements of Financial Accounting Standards Board in reporting financial information on a constant dollar and current cost basis. Constant dollar is the historical cost as inflated according to the consumer price index. Current cost represents the current actual value according to the assets remaining service potential at the measurement date.

Report content (for selected asset classes):

Fixed asset identification
Beginning balance
Additions
Retirements
Other changes
Ending balance

Totals for dollar values by classification, company, and location.

EXHIBIT F
Investment Tax Credit Reporting

Report usage:

To claim credit on current year's acquisitions and reporting recapture for those assets which have been disposed of prior to tax estimated life.

Report content (for current year acquisitions and retirements):

Fixed asset identification
Asset Class (1245 only)
New/used code
Acquisition date—year/month
Estimated life
Depreciation method
Cost
Calculated ITC amount
Disposition date—year/month

Note: Our organization uses the modified half-year first year convention.

180 FIXED ASSET ACCOUNTING

EXHIBIT G
Surplus Machinery and Equipment Report(s) by Category

Report usage:

A report generator or generalized inquiry feature would be an aid in preparing lists of:
1. Surplus equipment by class
2. Equipment "locator" lists by class

Report content (variable depending on use of the report) may include:

Fixed asset identification
Description
Tag number
Machine/equipment class
Surplus indicator
Acquisition cost
Current book value

EXHIBIT H
Property Tax Reporting

Report purpose:

Provide the proper identification and selection of fixed assets subject to property taxation by a *wide* variety of tax jurisdictions.

Report content:

Fixed asset identification
Location—city and state (tax jurisdiction)
Asset class—many codes may be required
Acquisition date and cost
Real or personal property identifier
Taxable or tax exempt identifier
Net book value

    F. Leased asset reporting, including automatic analysis under Financial Accounting Standards Board 13 requirements.
  4. Additional flexibility for:
    A. Maintaining data for multiple companies, divisions, and locations.
    B. Expanded classification and description of fixed assets.

C. Separate asset/depreciation reporting for book and tax purposes.
   D. Responding to changes in fixed asset and leased asset reporting requirements as dictated by management, government, or regulatory agencies in a timely, accurate manner.
5. Input to the general ledger system.

In addition, changes in the current capitalizing procedure should be made to ensure complete, consistent, and timely input to the fixed asset accounting system.

Benefits

I. About 1,800 accountant hours could be saved annually due to:
   1. More timely detection and correction of errors.
   2. Complete classification and coding of fixed assets for a variety of reporting functions.
   3. Automatic preparation of reports not currently available.
      A. Actual and projected depreciation and book values.
      B. ADR, FASB 33, ITC, and other governmental reporting aids.
      C. Surplus equipment, "locator lists", and other specific retrievals.
   4. Elimination of manually coding fixed asset input to the General Ledger system.
II. Improved control and utilization of fixed assets and leased assets through more comprehensive, accurate, and timely reports.
III. Reduce vulnerability under IRS and public accountant audits through improved accuracy, timeliness, and audit trail of reported data in compliance with government and Generally Accepted Accounting Procedures (GAAP) requirements.

Cost/Benefit Analysis—
Fixed Asset
Accounting System
September, 1981

INDEX

Introduction .... page 183
Alternatives 184
Acquisition and Maintenance Costs 185
Benefits 187
Recommendation 187

COST/BENEFIT ANALYSIS—FIXED ASSET ACCOUNTING SYSTEM

User Project Manager—John Smith
MIS Project Manager—James Doe
Date: 9/23/81

Introduction

The current fixed asset accounting system is inflexible, not comprehensive, and does not provide necessary information on a timely basis. Regulatory requirements have changed since it was written in 1970. On July 14, 1981, a Statement of Requirements for a new fixed system was presented to the MIS Steering Committee. The inadequacies of the present system as explained included:

1. Heavy manual effort in accounting, tax, and various engineering departments resulting in inefficiencies, error prone data, and timeliness problems.

COST/BENEFIT ANALYSIS

2. Extremely limited data base and inflexibility of data retrieval resulting in "guesstimates" on various tax reports and difficulties in controlling and maximizing utilization of existing fixed assets.
3. Duplication of effort to enter data in the Fixed Asset System and the General Ledger System because of a lack of interface between the two.

The MIS Steering Committee directed the project team to prepare a cost/benefit analysis for review. In this cost/benefit analysis, the value of anticipated benefits has been estimated by the user departments and the estimated costs were developed by MIS.

Alternatives

Option 1: Buy a package which uses our data base management facility.

A. No independent software vendor currently offers a software version which will interface with our data base product.
B. One vendor will offer an on-line updating version in 1982 at an additional cost of $10,000.00. A data base version is planned, but is number 3 in priority—at least 18 months away with no firm commitment.
C. It would be a major rewrite for remaining vendors to convert their sequential batch systems to a data base application. None were willing to undertake such a conversion to our current data base management system due to marketing priority and prohibitive costs.

Option 2: Modify an existing software package to run under our data base management system. (Recommended)

A. Most packages, after procurement, would be relatively easy to convert to our data base management system due to modular construction.
B. Most fixed asset packages generally require about one change per year. Enhancements or changes to these systems in reaction to government or regulatory agency requirements will have undergone CPA review prior to receipt by our organization. This assures adherence to IRS and Standard Accounting Procedures. Also, this will minimize MIS, Accounting, and Tax department personnel involvement in maintenance.
C. The software vendors, with their larger specialized staffs, can be expected to be able to react more quickly to outside agency dictated changes than our Accounting, Tax, and MIS departments could with an in-house developed system.
D. Due to modular construction, conversion changes to input/output modules should remain free of routine enhancement conflicts.

E. In keeping with our policy of minimizing the customization of purchased software, generally changes made to this system would be limited to those initiated by the vendor, and this would be within the scope of the vendors system's capabilities. However, this constraint is not anticipated to cause us a problem since we have identified only one reporting requirement that is unique to our organization.
F. The time to implement a system or enhancements to the system would be minimal—little development or in-house programming time would be required.

Option 3: Develop a system in-house making use of our data base management system capabilities.

A. Development and programming in-house may be more cost effective initially. Maintenance costs may also be less than package maintenance but would depend upon the size of enhancements made as a result of regulatory changes.
B. Other advantages of an in-house developed system in line with our data base management system environment are:
 1. On-line updating with instantaneous feedback.
 2. From the MIS viewpoint, it would be relatively easy to make changes to accommodate any unique organizational specifications and implement them according to our own desired schedule.
C. In-house development and maintenance would require more time from our employees in the Accounting, Tax, and MIS departments over a longer period of time. The installation date would depend upon manpower availability and the project management schedule in those departments.
D. The ability to effectively develop and maintain the desired system within the organization would require the contracting of outside professional assistance to review the system to insure compliance with IRS and FASB (Financial Accounting Standards Board). Additional training of MIS staff will be needed to determine some specific techniques such as table development for various calculations.

Acquisition and Maintenance Costs

Option 1: Buy a data base management system to fit our environment package. Not available as an option.

186 COST/BENEFIT ANALYSIS

Option 2: Convert a package to our data base management system.

Development	Low	High	Mean
Software	$16,000	$37,500	$30,833
Selection—4 people @ 20 hrs.	1,200	1,200	1,200
Training—4 people @ 24 hours.	1,440	1,440	1,440
Program conversion	2,600	12,350	3,638
Installation—2 persons @ 40 hrs.	1,140	1,140	1,140
Data preparation—2 @ 100 hrs.	2,000	2,000	2,000
Total	$24,380	$55,630	$40,296

Operational Costs	Low	High	Mean
Package maintenance	$1,600	$4,500	$3,646
Maintenance—100 hrs.—all	1,400	1,400	1,400
Computer charges estimated	1,500	1,500	1,500
	$4,500	$7,400	$6,546

Approximate installation target dates:

Selection	Nov. 20
Acquisition	Dec. 15
Conversion (begin in February)	March 5
Installation	March 19

Option 3: Develop a data base management version in-house.

Development	Hours	Costs
Specification/design—MIS	500	$ 6,500
Specification/design—other team members	300	4,500
Programming/testing	850	11,050
Training	96	1,440
Installation	80	1,140
Data preparation	200	2,000
Total	2,026	$26,630

Operational Costs	Hours	Cost
Maintenance—10% MIS development	135	$1,755
Maintenance—other team members	70	1,050
Computer charges		1,500
Total	205	$4,305

Approximate installation target dates:

Specification/design (entire team— after project initiation)	June 30
Programming/testing—2 people	Sept. 17
Installation	Sept. 30

Benefits

I. Dollarized Benefits

	Exempt Hours	Nonexempt Hours	Total Hours
Annual & long-range plans, budgets, forecasts	80	80	160
Reconciliation to General Ledger	20	80	100
Cash flow data	—	20	20
Duplicate entries	20	180	200
FASB 33 reporting	20	80	100
FASB 13/leased assets	125	75	200
Year end audit schedules	40	40	80
6330 quarterly report	—	60	60
Tax reporting	80	—	80
Surplus equipment listing	—	40	40
Ad hoc queries	60	—	60
Multigroup level reports	—	400	400
Complete updated monthly listing	—	200	200
Engineering savings	130	—	130
	575	1,255	1,830
Estimated dollar savings	$8,625	$10,668	$19,293

The above savings are based upon the estimated time needed to meet the mandatory and desired reporting requirements for our organization.

II. Improved control and utilization of fixed assets and leased assets through more comprehensive, accurate, and timely reports.

In addition to the above savings, a new computerized fixed asset system would improve accuracy of depreciation and asset budgeting, various federal, state, and local tax reports, and engineering and internal management reports. Without a sound system of accumulating, storing, calculating, and retrieving fixed asset data, "guesstimates" must be used in many cases. This is the opportune time to get control of these asset records to provide reports to engineering and plant managers to enable them to physically control and maximize effective utilization of this major investment.

III. Reduce vulnerability under IRS and public accountant audits through improved accuracy, timeliness, and audit trail of reported data in compliance with government and Financial Accounting Standards Board Requirements.

Recommendation

Considering all factors, the recommended option is the purchase of vendor software with conversion to our data base management system (Option 2).

Under this option, the utilization of limited personnel resources, both MIS and users, is minimized. The fixed asset reporting system requirements for our organization are not unique. Several packages available on the market can handle our needs. They are well-designed, modular systems which again minimize our effort to install changes as they are released by the vendor. This will enable us to direct more of our efforts toward those systems that do require a customized design.

The recent attention focused on fixed and leased assets, as a result of government and regulatory agencies directives on reporting requirements, has seen a rush of companies such as ours looking to fixed asset software vendors to help solve this problem. Because of the complexity of the interpretation of these accounting pronouncements and tax regulations, these software vendors regularly contract the services of CPA firms to insure their systems meet the needs of users in accordance with proper accounting and tax standards.

Based upon the assumption that MIS personnel resources would be available on February 1 to begin conversion of a system to our data base management system, we estimate it would be completely installed and ready to accept the loading of our historical data within two months—more than six months sooner than an in-house designed system. This six month difference is important for two reasons:

1. We are playing catch up! That is, our fixed asset system has been neglected for so long, while the complexities of the reporting needs have increased, that continued manual efforts alone leave us further behind.
2. We can utilize the new system to input all of calendar year 1982 activity by loading three months of history (March completion—Purchased package) much easier than we could load nine months of history (September completion—In-house developed system).

In summary, the statement of requirements explained the inadequacies of the present system. Because the present computer system is so poor, much manual effort is required to perform even the minimum reporting requirements. This, coupled with incompleteness of the data carried by the present system results in reporting inaccuracies, timeliness problems, and underutilization and control of our physical assets. In the past few weeks, the federal government's recently passed tax bill created a whole new set of complexities in tax accounting for our assets. It also adds a new potential for us to obtain cost advantages through sale/leaseback arrangements, thereby requiring us to account for capitalized leases for the first time.

The solution to this escalating problem requires a new, comprehensive fixed-asset system that incorporates tax and lease accounting features such as those presently available as software packages.

The recommended option makes optimum use of our personnel resources, outweighing the monetary difference. It is the quickest solution to a long-standing and rapidly worsening problem. By choosing a software vendor with experience in fixed- and leased-asset reporting systems, and a proven track record, we have a low-risk answer to increasingly complex requirements.

Index

A

Accelerated Depreciation Range (ADR), 175–177, 181
Automation
  accounting spread sheets, 95
  changes in technology, 40
  comfort level, 37
  office, 29–37
  office automation committee, 35
  rush to, 1
  understanding of benefits, 170–171

B

Bottom line
  issues, 6
  linkage to MIS effort, 15

C

Cathode Ray Tube (CRT)
  response times, 91–92
  use of, 12–13, 174
Change management, 172–173
Clients, 8
  complaints, 18
  number of, 19
  relationships, 17, 22, 27
  role of, 11
Computer
  controls, 128–130
  personal, 7
  utility, 100
Consultants
  outside, 70, 169
Corrupt Fair Practice Act, 147, 164
Cost benefit, 5
  analysis document, 60–62, 64
Credibility, 5, 66, 80
Crisis
  management, 14, 24
Cultural
  changes, 15
  differences, 18
  maturity, 56
  problems, 6, 24–25, 58

D

Data
  classifications, 150–151
  control of, 86–87, 148
  ownership, 159–160
  redundancy, 89, 153–154, 160
  security, 151–152, 162–163
  value of, 147–148
  vs. information, 11–12

192 INDEX

Data Base Administrator
  location within organization, 159
Data Base Management System (DBMS)
  availability of, 150–159
  introduction of, 150–159
  planning, 156
  recovery, 100–154
Data dictionary, 154, 157–158
Data entry
  elimination of central function, 36
Data processing
  lower cost, 4
  "stone age," 72–73
Disaster
  contingency planning, 43, 45–47, 164
    agreements, 53
    costs, 48–49
    details, 50–51
    examples of, 45–46
    offsite facilities, 51–52
    testing, 53
Documentation, 70–71, 78–79, 89–90
  information center requirements, 98

E

Equipment
  capability, 33
  selection, 33

F

Feasibility study, 56–59
Financial Accounting Standards Board (FASB), 175–177, 179–181

G

Generally Accepted Accounting Procedures (GAAP), 181

I

Information center, 83, 86, 88–92
  assessment of potential within the organization, 94
  champion, 93
  client responsibilities, 97–99
  hardware considerations, 99
  introduction, 95
  newsletter, 98
  presentation, 96
  threat to MIS power, 93

J

Jargon, 6, 25, 28

M

Management skills
  lack of, 9
  technical, 8
Manufacturing Requirements Planning (MRP), 58–59
Microprocessor
  availability of, 84
  growth of technology, 84
  link to mainframe, 39
MIS steering committee, 7, 35
  charter, 132, 143–145
  function, 131
  role of MIS manager, 135, 137
  structure, 132–134

P

Planning
  long range, 31–33, 79
Policies
  control of data processing hardware, 87–88
  office automation, 37–38
Political, 13
  aspects of office automation, 31
Programming languages
  cobol, 100
  high level, 12, 90–92, 155
  non-procedural, 12
  obsolete, 72
Project
  client responsibilities, 107–108
  contingency factor, 141
  costs of, 4
  data center involvement, 115
  evaluation, 56
  evaluation sheet, 139–140

implementation considerations, 116–118
management of, 104–107
overruns, 142
size considerations, 111–112
specifications
  detail, 114
  general, 113–114
standard project management, 106–107, 109–116
status reporting, 107

R

Risk
  associated with projects, 110–111
  assumption of, 68–73
  degree of, 2
  failure to accept, 14

S

Senior management
  awareness of need for contingency plan, 49
  commitment of, 6, 9–10
  communication with MIS, 26
  involvement, 25
  responsibility, 10
Service level, 23–24
Software
  "make or buy" considerations, 77
  obsolescence, 40
  operating complexity, 5
  purchased packages, 63–78
State of the art, 65–67, 75
  effect on MIS employee turnover, 79
  future effects, 167